LONDON SCENE

from

THE STRAND

Aspects of Victorian London culled from the Strand Magazine
selected and arranged by Gareth Cotterell

BOOK CLUB ASSOCIATES
London

This selection of articles originally appeared in the *Strand Magazine*

This edition published 1975 by Book Club Associates
by arrangement with Diploma Press

Printed in Great Britain
Photo-litho reprint by W & J Mackay Limited, Chatham

Contents

Introduction

The factual articles and features in the *Strand Magazine* mirrored society at all levels and in most facets from 1891 until well after the Second World War.

By close attention to the earlier issues of the Magazine and by a process of selection, I present in this book differing aspects of Victorian London, which together form a kind of unity.

These pieces involve scenes and institutions, some of which have amazingly survived till this day, even if much changed, while others have long vanished.

Victorian firemen, child workers, street musicians, lost dogs, artists, river policemen and street-corner men—all have disappeared with their shadows and into the shadows, yet they are indestructible if only because their descendants and successors can be seen in London today.

Gareth Cotterell
July 1974

Burly house

Harvue on the hill

Semerset house   Arundel house   Esex Stairs   Whitfryers Stairs

*The Strand from the Thames,
Sixteenth Century.*

The Story of the Strand.

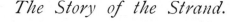

STRAND is a great
deal more than Lon-
don's most ancient
and historic street : it
is in many regards the
most interesting street
in the world. It has
not, like Whitehall or the Place de la
Concorde, seen the execution of a king ; it
has never, like the Rue de Rivoli, been
swept by grape-shot ; nor has it, like the
Antwerp Place de Meir, run red with
massacre. Of violent incident it has seen
but little ; its interest is the interest of
association and development. Thus it has
been from early Plantagenet days, ever
changing its aspect, growing from a river-
side bridle-path to a street of palaces, and
from the abiding-place of the great nobles,
by whose grace the king wore his crown, to
a row of shops about which there is nothing
that is splendid and little that is remarkable. It is not a fine street, and only here
and there is it at all striking or picturesque.
But now, as of yore, it is the high road between the two cities—puissant London and
imperial Westminster. From the days of
the Edwards to this latest moment it has
been the artery through which the tide of
Empire has flowed. Whenever England
has been victorious or has rejoiced, whenever she has been in sadness or tribulation,
the Strand has witnessed it all. It has been
filled with the gladness of triumph, the
brilliant mailed cavalcades that knew so
well how to ride down Europe ; filled, too,
with that historic procession which remains
the high water-mark of British pageantry,
in the midst of which the king came to his
own again. The tide of Empire has
flowed westward along the Strand for

generations which we may number but not
realise, and it remains to-day the most important, as it was once the sole, highway
between the two cities.

What the Strand looked like when it was
edged with fields, and the road, even now
not very wide, was a mere bridle-path, and
a painful one at that, they who know the
wilds of Connemara may best realise. From
the western gate of the city of London—a
small and feeble city as yet—to the Westminster Marshes, where already there was
an abbey, and where sometimes the king
held his court, was a long and toilsome
journey, with the tiny village of Charing for
halting-place midway. No palaces were
there ; a few cabins perhaps, and footpads
certainly. Such were the unpromising beginnings of the famous street which
naturally gained for itself the name of
Strand, because it ran along the river bank
—a bank which, be it remembered, came up
much closer than it does now, as we may
see by the forlorn and derelict water-gate of
York House, at the Embankment end of
Buckingham-street. Then by degrees, as
the age of the Barons approached, when
kings reigned by the grace of God, perhaps,
but first of all by favour of the peers, the
Strand began to be peopled by the salt of
the earth.

Then arose fair mansions, chiefly upon the
southern side, giving upon the river, for the
sake of the airy gardens, as well as of easy
access to the stream which remained London's
great and easy highway until long after the
Strand had been paved and rendered practic-
able for wheels. It was upon the water, then,
that the real pageant of London life—a fine
and well-coloured pageant it must often have
been—was to be seen. By water it was that

the people of the great houses went to their plots, their wooings, their gallant intrigues, to Court, or to Parliament. Also it was by water that not infrequently they went, by way of Traitor's Gate, to Tower Hill, or at least to dungeons which were only saved from being eternal by policy or expediency. This long Strand of palaces became the theatre of a vast volume of history which marked the rise and extension of some of the grandest houses that had been founded in feudal- ism, or have been built upon its ruins. Some of the fami- lies which lived there in power and pomp are mere memories now; but the names of many of them are still familiar in Belgravia as once they were in the Strand. There was, to start with, the original Somerset House, more pic- turesque, let us hope, than the depressing mauso- leum which now daily reminds us that man is mortal. Then there was the famous York House, nearer to Charing Cross, of which nothing but the water-gate is left. On the op- posite side of the way was Burleigh House, the home of the great states- man who, under God and Queen Elizabeth, did such great things for England. Bur- leigh is one of the earliest recorded cases of a man being killed by over-work. " Ease and pleasure," he sighed, while yet he was under fifty, " quake to hear of death ; but my life, full of cares and miseries, desireth to be dissolved." The site of Burleigh House is kept in memory, as those of so many other of the vanished palaces of the Strand, by a street named after it ; and the office of this magazine stands no doubt upon a part of Lord Burleigh's old garden. When

1890
The Strand
as we know it,
looking west

Southampton House, Essex House, the Palace of the Savoy, and Northumber- land House, which disappeared so lately, are added, we have still mentioned but a few of the more famous of the Strand houses.

But the Strand is distinguished for a vast deal more than that. Once upon a time, it was London's Belgravia. It was never perhaps the haunt of genius, as the Fleet- street tributaries were ; it was never an Alsatia, as Whitefriars was, nor had it the many interests of the City itself. But it had a little of all these things, and the result is that the interest of the Strand is unique. It would be easy to spend a long day in the Strand and its tributaries, search- ing for landmarks of other days, and visiting sites which have long been historic. But the side streets are, if anything, more in- teresting than the main thoroughfare, and they deserve a special and sepa- rate visit, when the mile or so of road-way between what was Temple Bar and Charing Cross has been ex- hausted. Could Londoners of even only a hundred years ago see the Strand as we know it, they would be very nearly as much surprised as a Cockney under the Plantagenets, who should have re-visited his London in the time of the Georges. They who knew the picturesque but ill-kept London of the Angevin sovereigns found the Strand a place of torment.

In 1353 the road was so muddy and so full of ruts that a commissioner was appointed to repair it at the expense of the frontagers. Even towards the end of Henry VIII.'s reign it was "full of pits and

SNOW'S BANK : FROM A SKETCH, 1808.

ing their swords and shouting with inexpressible joy ; the way strew'd with flowers, the bells ringing, the streets hung with tapestry, fountains running with wine ; the mayor, aldermen, and all the companies in their liveries, chains of gold, and banners ; lords and nobles clad in cloth of silver, gold, and velvet ; the windows and balconies well set with ladies ; trumpets, music, and myriads of people. . . . They were eight hours passing the city, even from two till ten at night. I stood in the Strand, and beheld it, and bless'd God." A century earlier Elizabeth had gone in state to St. Paul's, to return thanks for the destruction of the Armada. Next, Queen Anne went in triumph up to St. Paul's, after Blenheim ; and, long after, the funeral processions of Nelson and Wellington were added to the list of great historic sights which the Strand has seen. The most recent of these great processions was the Prince of Wales's progress of thanksgiving to St. Paul's in 1872.

Immediately we leave what was Temple Bar, the Strand's memories begin. We have made only a few steps from Temple Bar, when we come to a house—No. 217, now a branch of the London and Westminster Bank—which, after a long and respectable history, saw its owners at length overtaken by shame and ruin. It was the banking-house of Strahan, Paul & Bates, which had been founded by one Snow and his partner Walton in Cromwell's days. In the beginning the house was "The Golden Anchor," and Messrs. Strahan & Co. have among their archives ledgers (kept in decimals !) which go back to the time of Charles II.

In 1855 it was discovered that some of the partners had been using their customers' money for their own pleasures or necessities. The guilty persons all went to prison ; one of the few instances in which, as in the case of Fauntleroy, who was hanged for forgery, English bankers have been convicted of breach of trust. Adjoining this house is that of Messrs. Twining, who opened, in 1710, the first tea-shop in London. They still deal in tea, though fine ladies no longer go to the Eastern

sloughs, very perilous and noisome." Yet it was by this miserable road that Cardinal Wolsey, with his great and stately retinue, passed daily from his house in Chancery-lane to Westminster Hall. In that respect there is nothing in the changed condition of things to regret ; but we may, indeed, be sorry for this : that there is left, save in its churches, scarcely a brick of the old Strand.

Still there are memories enough, and for these we may be thankful. Think only of the processions that have passed up from Westminster to St. Paul's, or the other way about ! Remember that wonderful cavalcade amid which Charles II. rode back from his Flemish exile to the palace which had witnessed his father's death. Nothing like it has been seen in England since. Evelyn has left us a description of the scene, which is the more dramatic for being brief : "May 29, 1660. This day His Majesty Charles II. came to London, after a sad and long exile and calamitous suffering, both of the King and Church, being seventeen years. This was also his birthday, and, with a triumph above 20,000 horse and foot, brandish-

Strand in their carriages to drink it, out of curiosity, at a shilling a cup.

One of the most interesting buildings in Essex-street, the "Essex Head" tavern, has only just been pulled down. There it was that Dr. Johnson founded "Sam's" Club, so named after the landlord, Samuel Graves. Dr. Johnson himself drew up the rules of the club, as we may see in Boswell's "Life." The chair in which he is reported to have sat was preserved in the house to the end. It is now cared for at the "Cheshire Cheese" in Fleet-street. A very redoubtable gentleman who formerly lived in Essex-street was Dr. George Fordyce, who for twenty years drank daily with his dinner a jug of strong ale, a quarter of a pint of brandy, and a bottle of port. And he was able to lecture to his students afterwards!

Nearly opposite Essex-street stands one of the most famous of London landmarks—the church of St. Clement Danes. Built as recently as 1682, it is the successor of a far older building. Its most interesting association is with Dr. Johnson, whose pew in the north gallery is still reverently kept, and an inscription marks the spot. In this church too, it was that Miss Davies, the heiress, who brought the potentiality of untold wealth into the family of the Grosvenors, was married to the progenitor of the present Duke of Westminster. St. Clement Danes is one of the few English churches with a *carillon*, which is of course set to psalm tunes. Milford-lane, opposite, was once really a lane with a bridge over a little stream which emptied into the Thames. Later on it marked the boundary of Arundel House, the home of the Dukes of Norfolk, who have built Arundel, Norfolk, Howard, and Surrey streets upon its site. In the time of Edward VI. the Earl of Arundel bought the property for forty pounds, which would seem to have been a good bargain even for those days. In Arundel House died "old Parr," who, according to the inscription upon his tomb in Westminster Abbey, lived to be 152 years old. Happily for himself he had lived all his life in Shropshire, and the brief space that he spent in London killed him.

The streets that have been built upon the site of old Arundel House are full of interesting associations. The house at the south-western corner of Norfolk and Howard-streets—it is now the "Dysart Hotel"—has a very curious history. A former owner—it was some sixty years since—was about to be married. The wedding breakfast was laid out in a large room on the first floor, and all was ready, except the lady, who changed her mind at the last minute. The jilted bridegroom locked up the banquet-chamber, put the key in his pocket, and, so the

1890
St Clement Danes

story runs, never again allowed it to be entered. There, it was said, still stood such mouldering remains of the wedding breakfast as the rats and mice had spared. Certainly the window curtains could for many years be seen crumbling to pieces, bit by bit, and the windows looked exactly as one would expect the windows of the typical haunted chamber to look. It is only of late that the room has been re-opened. The name of the supposed hero of this story has often been mentioned, but, since the story may quite possibly be baseless, it would be improper to repeat it. But there is no doubt whatever that for nearly half a century there was something very queer about that upper chamber.

This same Howard-street was the scene, in 1692, shortly after it was built, of a tragedy which remained for generations in the popular memory. It took place within two or three doors of the " Dysart Hotel." The central figure of the pitiful story was Mrs. Bracegirdle, the famous and beautiful actress. One of her many admirers, Captain Richard Hill, had offered her marriage, and had been refused. But he was not to be put off in that way. If he could not obtain the lady by fair means he was determined to get her by force. He therefore resolved, with the assistance of Lord Mohun—a notorious person, who was afterwards killed in Hyde-park in a duel with the Duke of Hamilton—to carry her off.

1890 St Marys-le-Strand

Geo-C-Haite

They stationed a coach in Drury-lane, and attempted to kidnap her as she was passing down the street after the play. The lady's screams drew such a crowd that the abductors were forced to bid their men let her go. They escorted her home (a sufficiently odd proceeding in the circumstances), and then remained outside Mrs. Bracegirdle's house in Howard-street " vowing revenge," the contemporary accounts say, but against whom is not clear. Hill and Lord Mohun drank a bottle of wine in the middle of the street, perhaps to keep their courage up, and presently Mr. Will Mountfort, an actor, who lived in Norfolk-street, came along. Mountfort had already heard what had happened, and he at once went up to Lord Mohun (who, it is said, " embraced him very tenderly "), and reproached him with " justifying the rudeness of Captain Hill," and with " keeping company with such a pitiful fellow." " And then," according to the Captain's servant, " the Captain came forward and said he would justify himself, and went towards the middle of the street and drew." Some of the eye-witnesses said that they fought, but others declared that Hill ran Mountfort through the body before he could draw his sword. At all events, Hill instantly ran away, and when the watch arrived they found only Lord Mohun, who surrendered himself. He seems to have had no part in the murder, and his sword was still sheathed when he was made prisoner. It is said that

Hill already had a grudge against Mountfort, whom he suspected of being Mrs. Bracegirdle's favoured lover. But the best contemporary evidence agrees that the lady's virtue was "as impregnable as the rock of Gibraltar."

Nearly opposite the scene of this brutal tragedy, the church of St. Mary-le-Strand was built some five-and-twenty years later. It is a picturesque building, and makes a striking appearance when approached from the west. It has of late been more than once proposed that it should be demolished, at once by reason of the obstruction which it causes in the roadway, and because of its ill-repair. But since it has now been put into good condition, the people who would so gaily pull down a church to widen a road will perhaps not be again heard from. According to Hume, Prince Charles Edward, during his famous stolen visit to London, formally renounced in this church the Roman Catholic religion, to strengthen his claim to the throne ; but there has never been any manner of proof of that statement. The site of St. Mary-le-Strand was long famous as the spot upon which the Westminster maypole stood, and what is now Newcastle-street was called Maypole-lane down to the beginning of the present century. At the Restoration, a new maypole, 134 feet high, was set up, the Cromwellians having destroyed the old one, in the presence of the King and the Duke of York. The pole is said to have been spliced together with iron bands by a blacksmith named John Clarges, whose daughter Anne married General Monk, who, for his services in bringing about the Restoration, was created Duke of Albemarle. Three or four suits were brought to prove that her first husband was still living when she married the Duke, and that consequently the second (and last) Duke of Albemarle was illegitimate, but the blacksmith's daughter gained them all. Near the Olympic Theatre there still exists a Maypole-alley.

It is hardly necessary to say that the present Somerset House, which is exactly opposite the church of St. Mary-le-Strand, is not the original building of that name. People—praise to their taste !—did not build in that fashion in the time of the Tudors. The old house, built by not the cleanest means, by the Protector Somerset, was "such a palace as had not been seen in England." After Somerset's attainder it became the recognised Dower House of the English Queens. It was built with the materials of churches and other people's houses. John of Padua was the architect, and it was a sumptuous palace indeed ; but if Somerset ever lived in it, it was for a very brief space. One of the accusations upon which he was attainted was that he had spent money in building Somerset House, but had allowed the King's soldiers to go unpaid. It was close to the Water Gate of Somerset House that the mysterious murder of Sir Edmundbury Godfrey took place in 1678. The story of the murder is so doubtful and complicated that it is impossible to enter upon it here. Sir Edmundbury was induced to go to the spot where he was strangled under the pretence that, as a justice of the peace, he could stop a quarrel that was going on. Titus Oates, the most finished scoundrel ever born on British soil,

SOMERSET HOUSE : FROM A DRAWING BY S. WALE, 1776.

suggested that the Jesuits and even Queen Henrietta Maria were concerned in instigating the murder, and three men were hung at Tyburn for their supposed share in it. Around the Somerset House of that day there were extensive gardens of that square formal fashion which, although pleasing enough to the antiquary, are anathema to the artistic eye. Old Somerset House was demolished in the early days of George III., and the present building, of which Sir Wm. Chambers was the architect, was commenced in 1776.

Another interesting bit of the southern side of the Strand is the region still called The Savoy. The old Palace of the Savoy was built by Simon de Montfort, but it afterwards passed to Peter of Savoy, uncle of Queen Eleanor, who gave to the precinct the name which was to become historical. There it was that King John of France was housed after he was taken prisoner at Poictiers ; and there too he died. The Palace of the Savoy was set on fire and plundered by Wat Tyler and his men in 1381. It was rebuilt and turned into a hospital by Henry VII. In the new building the liturgy of the Church of England was revised after the restoration of Charles II. ; but the most interesting association of the place must always be that there Chaucer wrote a portion of the "Canterbury Tales," and that John of Ghent lived there. After many vicissitudes and long ruin and neglect, the last remains of the Palace and Hospital of the Savoy were demolished at the beginning of the present century, to permit of a better approach to Waterloo Bridge.

A little farther west, in Beaufort-buildings, Fielding once resided. A contemporary tells how he was once hard put to it to pay the parochial taxes for this house. The tax-collector at last lost patience, and Fielding was compelled to obtain an advance from Jacob Tonson, the famous publisher, whose shop stood upon a portion of the site of Somerset House. He returned home with ten or twelve guineas in his pocket, but meeting at his own door an old college chum who had fallen upon evil times, he emptied his pockets, and was unable to

satisfy the tax-gatherer until he had paid a second visit to the kindly and accommodating Tonson. Another of the great Strand palaces stood on this site—Worcester House, which, after being the residence of the Bishops of Carlisle, became the town house of the Earls of Worcester. Almost adjoining stood Salisbury, or Cecil House, which was built by Robert Cecil, first Earl of Salisbury, a son of the sage Lord Burghley, whose town house stood on the opposite side of the Strand. It was pulled down more than two hundred years ago, after a very brief existence, and Cecil and Salisbury streets were built upon its site. Yet another Strand palace, Durham House, the "inn" of the Bishops Palatine of Durham, stood

COUTTS' BANKING HOUSE, 1853: FROM A DRAWING BY T. HOSMER SHEPHERD.

a little nearer to Charing Cross. It was of great antiquity, and was rebuilt as long ago as 1345. Henry VIII. obtained it by exchange, and Queen Elizabeth gave it to Sir Walter Raleigh. The most interesting event that ever took place in the house was the marriage of Lady Jane Grey to Lord Guildford Dudley. Eight weeks later she was proclaimed Queen, to her sorrow. Still nearer to Charing Cross, and upon a portion of the site of Durham House, is the famous bank of the Messrs. Coutts, one of the oldest of the London banks. The original Coutts was a shrewd Scotchman, who, by his wit and enterprise, speedily became rich and famous. He married one of his brother's domestic servants, and of that marriage, which turned out very happily, Lady Burdett-Coutts is a grandchild. Mr. Coutts' second wife was Miss Harriet Mellon, a distinguished actress of her day, to whom he left the whole of his fortune of £900,000. When the lady, who afterwards became Duchess of St. Albans, died in the year of the Queen's accession, that £900,000 formed the foundation of the great fortune of Miss Angela Burdett, better known to this generation as Lady Burdett-Coutts. Messrs. Coutts' banking-house is an interesting building, with many portraits of the early friends and customers of the house, which included Dr. Johnson and Sir Walter Scott. The cellars of the firm are reputed to be full of boxes containing coronets and patents of nobility. Upon another part of the site of Durham House the brothers Adam built, in 1768, the region called the Adelphi. There, in the centre house of Adelphi-terrace, with its wondrous view up and down the river, died in 1779 David Garrick.

Buckingham-street and Villiers-street, which lie between the Adelphi and Charing Cross Station, carry their history, like so many other of the Strand tributaries, written in their names. They recall the long-vanished glories of Villiers, Duke of Buckingham, who lived at York House, so called as having been the town palace of the Archbishops of York. Wolsey lived there for a time ; Bacon was living there when he was degraded. The Crown granted it to George Villiers, Duke of Buckingham, by whom it was splendidly rebuilt. The second Duke sold it to pay his debts, making it a condition that he should be commemorated in the names of the streets placed on the site—George, Villiers, Duke, and Buckingham streets. The only remaining relic of York House is the fine water-gate at the bottom of Buckingham-street. Close to this water-gate, in a house marked by a Society of Arts tablet, for a short time lived Peter the Great; opposite lived Samuel Pepys ; and No. 14 was occupied by Etty. In Villiers-street both Evelyn and Steele lived ; but it is now the haunt of anything rather than genius. Northumberland House, the last and best known of the riverside palaces, which was demolished only at the end of 1874,

1890
Burleigh Street

Geo G. Hrite 1890

1890
A First Night
at the Lyceum

Geo. C. Haite 1890

streets, was the house from which he governed England with conspicuous courage, devotion, and address. There, too, he was visited by Queen Elizabeth. According to tradition she wore, on that occasion, the notorious pyramidal head-dress which she made fashionable, and was besought by an esquire in attendance to stoop as she entered. "For your master's sake I will stoop, but not for the King of Spain," was the answer which might have been expected from a daughter of Henry VIII. Lord Burleigh lived there in considerable state, spending thirty pounds a week, which in Elizabethan days was enormous. There, broken with work and anxiety, he died in 1598. When his son was made Earl of Exeter he called it Exeter House. This historical house was not long in falling upon evil days. By the beginning of the eighteenth century a part of it had been demolished, while another part was altered and turned into shops, the new building being christened "Exeter Change." Nearer to our own time the "Change" became a kind of arcade, the upper floor being used as a wild-beast show. When it was "Pidcock's Exhibition of Wild Beasts" an imitation Beef-eater stood outside, in the Strand, inviting the cockney and his country cousin to "walk up." The roaring of the animals is said to have often frightened horses in the Strand. "Exeter Change" was the home of "Chunee," an elephant as famous in his generation—it was more than sixty years since—as "Jumbo" in our own. "Chunee," which weighed five tons, and was eleven feet high, at last became unmanageable, and was shot by a file of soldiers, who fired 152 bullets into his body before killing him. His skeleton is still in the Museum of the College of Surgeons, in Lincoln's-inn-fields. It should be remembered that in Exeter-street Dr. Johnson lodged (at a cost of 4½d. per day) when he began his struggle in London. A little farther east once stood Wimbledon House, built some three centuries ago by Sir Edward Cecil, Viscount Wimbledon, a cadet of the great house founded by Lord Burleigh. Stow records that the house was burned down in 1628, the day after an accidental explosion

was not, properly speaking, in the Strand at all. It may therefore be sufficient to recall that it was built in 1605, and became the home of the Percies in 1642. It was sold to the Metropolitan Board of Works, with great and natural reluctance, for half a million of money ; and the famous blue lion of the Percies, which for so long stood proudly over the building, was removed to Sion House.

The northern side of the Strand is not quite so rich in memories as the side which faced the river, but its associations with Lord Burleigh, that calm, sagacious, and untiring statesman, must always make it memorable. Burleigh House, the site of which is marked by Burleigh and Exeter-

of gunpowder demolished the owner's country seat at Wimbledon. Nearly all the land hereabouts still belongs to the Cecils. Upon a portion of the site of Wimbledon House arose the once famous "D'Oyley's Warehouse," where a French refugee sold a variety of silk and woollen fabrics, which were quite new to the English market. He achieved great success, and a " D'Oyley " is still as much a part of the language as an " antimacassar "—that abomination of all desolation. The shop lasted, at 346, Strand, until some thirty years ago. The Lyceum Theatre, which also stands upon a piece of the site of Exeter House, occupies the spot where Madame Tussaud's waxworks were first exhibited in 1802.

With Bedford House, once the home of the Russells, which stood in what is now Southampton-street, we exhaust the list of the Strand palaces. There is but little to say of it, and it was pulled down in 1704. Southampton-street—so called after Rachel, the heroic wife of Wm. Lord Russell, who was a daughter of Thomas, Earl of Southampton—Tavistock-street, and some others were built upon its site. It was in Southampton-street that formerly stood the " Bedford Head," a famous and fashionable eating-house. Pope asks :—

> " When sharp with hunger, scorn you to be fed,
>   Except on pea-chicks at the ' Bedford Head ' ? "

He who loves his London, more especially he who loves his Strand, will not forget that No. 332, now the office of the *Weekly Times*, was the scene of Dickens' early work in journalism for the *Morning Chronicle*.

It would be impossible to find a street more entirely representative of the development of England than the long and not very lovely Strand. From the days of feudal fortresses to those of penny newspapers is a far cry ; and of all that lies between it has been the witness. If its stones be not historic, at least its sites and its memories are ; and still it remains, what it ever has been, the most characteristic and distinctive of English highways.

The Metropolitan Fire Brigade.

ITS HOME AND ITS WORK.

IRE! Fire!"
This startling cry aroused
me one night as I was putting
the finishing touches to some
literary work. Rushing, pen
in hand, to the window, I
could just perceive a dull red glare in the
northern sky, which, even as I gazed, became
more vivid, and threw some chimneys near
at hand into strong relief. A fire undoubt-
edly, and not far distant!

The street, usually so quiet at night, had
suddenly awakened. The alarm which had
reached me had aroused my neighbours on
each side of the way, and every house was

CAPTAIN SHAW.

"well alight" in a short space of time.
Doors were flung open, windows raised,
white forms were visible at the casements,
and curiosity was rife. Many men and some
venturesome women quitted their houses,
and proceeded in the direction of the glare,
which was momentarily increasing, the glow
on the clouds waxing and waning according
as the flames shot up or temporarily died
down.

"Where is it?" people ask in a quick,
panting way, as they hurry along. No one
can say for certain. But just as we think it
must be in Westminster, we come in sight

of a huge column of smoke, and turning a
corner are within view of the emporium—
a tall, six-storied block, stored with inflam-
mable commodities, and blazing fiercely.
Next door, or rather the next warehouse,
is not yet affected.

The scene is weird and striking; the
intense glare, the shooting flames which
dart viciously out and upwards, the white
and red faces of the crowd kept back by the
busy police, the puff and clank of the engines, the rushing and hissing of the water,
the roar of the fire, and the columns of
smoke which in heavy sulky masses hung
gloating over the blazing building. The
bright helmets of the firemen are glinting
everywhere, close to the already tottering
wall, on the summit of the adjacent buildings, which are already smoking. Lost on
ladders, amid smoke, they pour a torrent of
water on the burning and seething premises.
Above all the monotonous "puff, puff" of
the steamer is heard, and a buzz of admiration ascends from the attentive, silent crowd.

Suddenly arises a yell—a wild, unearthly
cry, which almost makes one's blood run cold
even in that atmosphere. A tremor seizes
us as a female form appears at an upper
window, framed in flame, curtained with
smoke and noxious fumes.

"Save her! Save her!"

The crowd sways and surges; women
scream; strong men clench their hands and
swear—Heaven only knows why. But before the police have headed back the people
the escape is on the spot, two men are on
it, one outstrips his mate, and darting up
the ladder, leaps into the open window.

He is swallowed up in a moment—lost to
our sight. Will he ever return out of that
fiery furnace? Yes, here he is, bearing a
senseless female form, which he passes out
to his mate, who is calmly watching his
progress, though the ladder is in imminent
danger. Quick! The flames approach!

The man on the ladder does not wait as
his mate again disappears and emerges with
a child about fourteen. Carrying this
burthen easily, he descends the ladder. The
first man is already flying down the escape,
head-first, holding the woman's dress round
her feet. The others, rescuer and rescued,
follow. The ladder is withdrawn, burning.

A mighty cheer arises 'mid the smoke. Two lives saved! The fire is being mastered. More engines gallop up. "The Captain" is on the spot, too. The Brigade is victorious.

In the early morning hour, as I strolled home deep in thought, I determined to see these men who nightly risk their lives and stalwart limbs for the benefit and preservation of helpless fire-scorched people. Who are these men who go literally through fire and water to assist and save their fellow creatures, strangers to them—unknown, save in that they require help and succour?

I determined there and then to see these brave fellows in their daily work, or leisure in their homes, amid all the surroundings of their noble calling. I went accompanied by an artistic friend, to whose efforts the illustrations which accompany this record are due.

Emerging from Queen-street, we find ourselves upon Southwark Bridge, and we at once plunge into a flood of memories of old friends who come, invisibly, to accompany us on our pilgrimage to old Winchester House, now the head-quarters of the Metropolitan Fire Brigade, in the Southwark Bridge-road. On the bridge—once a "tolled" structure known as the Iron Bridge—we find "Little Dorrit" herself, and her suitor, young John Chivery, in all his brave attire; the young aspirant is downhearted at the decided refusal of Miss Amy to marry him, as they pace the then almost unfrequented bridge. Their ghosts cross it in our company, with Clennan and Maggie behind us, till we reach the Union-road, once known as Horsemonger-lane, where young John's ghost quits us to meditate in the back yard of Mr. Chivery's premises, and become that "broken-down ruin," catching cold beneath the family washing, which he feared.

The whole neighbourhood is redolent of Dickens. From a spot close by the head office we can see the buildings which have been erected on the site of the King's Bench Prison, where Mr. Micawber waited for something to turn up, and where Copperfield lost his box and money. The site of the former "haven of domestic tranquillity and peace of mind," as Micawber styled it, is indicated to us by Mr. Harman—quite a suitable name in such a connection with Dickens—by whom we are courteously and pleasantly received in the office of the Metropolitan Fire Brigade.

Our credentials being in order there is no difficulty experienced in our reception. Nothing can exceed the civility and politeness of the officials, and of the rank and file of the Brigade. Fine, active, cheerful fellows, all sailors, these firemen are a credit to their organisation and to London. The Superintendent hands us over to a bright young fellow, who is waiting his promotion—we hope he has reached it, if not a death vacancy—and he takes us in charge kindly.

Standing in the very entrance, we had already remarked two engines. The folding, automatic doors are closed in front of these machines. One, a steamer, is being nursed by means of a gas tube to keep the fire-box warm. When the fire-call rings there is no time to begin to get up steam. The well-heated interior soon acts in response to the quickly lighted fire as the engine starts, and by the time our steamer reaches its destination steam is generated. A spare steamer is close at hand.

ENGINES GALLOP UP.

Very bright and clean is the machine, which in a way puts its useful ally, the " manual," in the shade ; though at present the latter kind are more numerous, in the proportion of seventy-eight to forty-eight. Turning from the engines, we notice a row of burnished helmets hanging over tunics, and below these, great knee-boots, which are so familiar to the citizen. When the alarm is rung, these are donned rapidly ; but we opine the gates will occupy some time in the opening.

Our guide smiles, and points out two ropes hanging immediately over the driving seat of each engine.

" When the engine is ready the coachman pulls the rope, and the gates open of their own accord, you may say. See here ! "

He turns to the office entrance, where two ropes are hanging side by side. A pull on each, and the doors leading to the backyard open and unfold themselves. The catch drops deftly into an aperture made to receive it, and the portals are thus kept open. About a second and a half is occupied in this manœuvre.

We consider it unfortunate that we shall not see a " turn out," as alarms by day are not usual. The Superintendent looks quizzical, but says nothing then. He gives instructions to our guide to show us all we want to see, and in this spirit we examine the instrument room close at hand.

Here are fixed a number of telephonic apparatus, labelled with the names of the stations :—Manchester-square, Clerkenwell, Whitechapel, and so on, five in number, known by the Brigade as Superintendents' Stations, A, B, C, D, E Districts. By these means immediate communication can be obtained with any portion of the Metropolis, and the condition and requirements of the fires reported. There is also a frame in the outer office which bears a number of electric bells, which can summon the head of any department, or demand the presence of any officer instantly.

It is extraordinary to see the quiet way in which the work is performed, the ease and freedom of the men, and the strict observance of discipline withal. Very few men are visible as we pass on to the repairing shops. (Illustration, p. 29.) Here the engines are repaired and inspected. There are eleven steamers in the shed, some available for service, and so designated. If an outlying station require a steamer in substitution for its own, here is one ready.

The boilers are examined every six months, and tested by water-pressure up to 180 lbs. on the square inch, in order to sustain safely the steam pressure up to 120 lbs., when it " blows off."

Passing down the shed we notice the men—all Brigade men—employed at their various tasks in the forge or carpenters' shop. Thus it will be perceived that the head-quarters enclose many different artizans, and is self-contained. The men were lifting a boiler when we were present, and our artist " caught them in the act."

Close to the entrance is a high " shoot " in which hang pendant numerous ropes and many lengths of drying hose. The impression experienced when standing underneath, and gazing upwards, is something like the feeling one would have while gazing up at the tops of the trees in a pine wood. There is a sense of vastness in this narrow lofty brick enclosure, which is some 70 ft. high. The hose is doubled in its length of 100 ft., and then it drains dry, for the moisture is apt to conceal itself in the rubber lining, and in the nozzles and head-screws of the hoses.

No precaution is neglected, no point is missed. Vigilant eyes are everywhere ; bright responsive faces and ready hands are continually in evidence, but unobtrusively.

Turning from the repairing shops we proceed to the stables, where we find things in the normal condition of preparedness. " Be ready " is evidently the watchword of the Brigade. Ready, aye ready ! Neatness and cleanliness are here scrupulously regarded. Tidiness is the feature of the stables. A pair of horses on either side are standing, faces outward, in their stalls. Four handsome, well-groomed, lithe animals they look ; and as we enter they regard us with considerable curiosity, a view which we reciprocate.

Round each horse's neck is suspended his collar. A weight let into the woodwork or the stall holds the harness by means of a lanyard and swivel. When the alarm rings the collar is dropped, and in " half a second " the animals, traces and splinter-bar hanging on their sleek backs and sides, are trotted out and harnessed. Again we express our regret that no kind householder will set fire to his tenement, that no nice children will play with matches or candle this fine morning, and let us " see everything," like Charles Middlewick.

Once more our guide smiles, and passes on through the forage and harness-rooms,

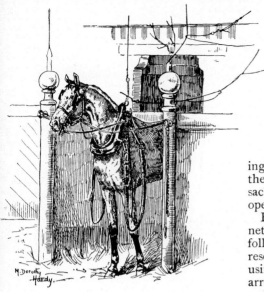

IN THE STABLES.

where we also find a coachman's room for reading, and waiting on duty.

It is now nearly mid-day, and we turn to see the fire-drill of the recruits, who, clad in slops, practise all the necessary and requisite work which alone can render them fit for the business. They are thus employed from nine o'clock to mid-day, and from two till four p.m. During these five hours the squads are exercised in the art of putting the ladders and escapes on the wagons which convey them to the scene of the fire. The recruit must learn how to raise the heavy machine by his own efforts, by means of a rope rove through a ring-bolt. We had an opportunity to see the recruits raising the machine together to get it off the wagon. The men are practised in leaping up when the vehicle is starting off at a great pace after the wheels are manned to give an impetus to the vehicle which carries such a burthen.

But the "rescue drill" is still more interesting, and this exhibited the strength and dexterity of the firemen in a surprising manner. It is striking to notice the different ways in which the rescue of the male and female sexes is accomplished. The sure-footed fireman rapidly ascends the ladder, and leaps upon the parapet. The escape is furnished with a ladder which projects beyond the net. At the bottom a canvas

sheet or "hammock" is suspended, so that the rescued shall not suffer from contusions, which formerly were frequent in consequence of the rapid descent.

One fireman passes into a garret window and emerges with a man. He makes no pause on the parapet, where already, heedless of glare and smoke and the risk of a fall, he has raised on his shoulders the heavy, apparently inanimate, form, and grasping the man round one leg, his arm inside the thigh, he carries him steadily, like a sack of coals, down the ladder as far as the opening of the bag-net of the escape. Here he halts, and puts the man into the net, perhaps head downwards, he himself following in the same position. The man rescued is then let down easily, the fireman using his elbows and knees as "breaks" to arrest their progress. So the individual is assisted down, and not permitted to go unattended.

The rescue of a female is accomplished in a slightly different manner. She is also carried to the ladder, but the rescuer grasps both her legs below the knees, and when he reaches the net he places her head downwards and grasps her dress tightly round her ankles, holding her thus in a straight position. Thus her dress is undisturbed, and she is received in the folds of the friendly canvas underneath, in safety.

There is also a "jumping drill" from the windows into a sheet held by the other men. This course of instruction is not so

FIRE ESCAPES

RECRUITS DRILLING.

popular, for it seems somewhat of a trial to leap in cold blood into a sheet some twenty feet below. The feat of lifting a grown man (weighing perhaps sixteen

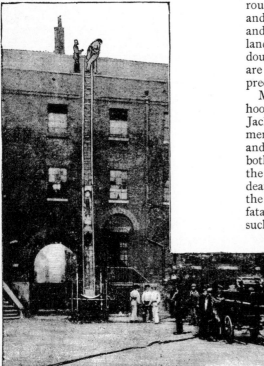

RESCUE DRILL.

stone) from the parapet to the right knee, then, by grasping the waist, getting the limp arm around his neck, and then, holding the leg, to rise up and walk on a narrow ledge amid all the terrible surroundings of a fire, requires much nerve and strength. Frequently we hear of deaths and injuries to men of the Brigade, but no landsman can attain proficiency in even double the time that sailors do—the latter are so accustomed to giddy heights, and to precarious footing.

Moreover, the belt, to which a swivel hook is attached, is a safeguard of which Jack takes every advantage. This equipment enables him to hang on to a ladder and swing about like a monkey, having both hands free to save or assist a victim or the fire or one of his mates. There is a death-roll of about five men annually, on the average, and many are injured, if not fatally yet very seriously, by falling walls and such accidents. Drenched and soaked, the men have a terrible time of it at a fire, and they richly deserve the leisure they obtain.

This leisure is, however, not so pleasant as might be imagined, for the fireman is always on duty; and, no matter how he is occupied, he may be wanted on the engine, and must go.

Having inspected the American ladder in its shed, we glanced at the stores and pattern rooms, and at the firemen's quarters. Here the men live with their wives and families, if they are married, and in single blessedness, if Love the Pilgrim has not come their way. Old Winchester House, festooned with creepers, was never put to more worthy use than in sheltering these retiring heroes, who daily risk their lives uncomplainingly. Somewhat different now the scenes from those when the stately palace of Cardinal Beaufort extended to the river, and the spacious park was stocked with game and venison. As our conductor seeks a certain key we muse on the old time, the feasts and pageants held here, the wedding banquet of James and Jane Somerset, when the old walls and precincts rang with merry cheer. Turning, we can almost fancy we perceive the restless Wyatt quitting the

pad we see all that remains of the brave Fireman JACOBS, who perished at the conflagration in Wandsworth in September, 1889.

It was on the 12th of that month that the premises occupied by Messrs. Burroughs and Wellcome, manufacturing chemists, took fire. Engineer Howard and two third-class firemen, Jacobs and Ashby, ran the hose up the staircase at the end of the building. The two latter men remained, but their retreat was suddenly cut off, and exit was sought by the window. The united ladder-lengths would not reach the upper story, and a builder's ladder came only within a few feet of the casement at which the brave men were standing calling for a line.

Ashby, whose helmet is still preserved, was fortunately able to squeeze himself through the bars, drop on the high ladder,

A SAD RECORD.

postern-gate, leaving fragments of the mutilated books of Winchester's proud bishop. These past scenes vanish as our guide returns and beckons us to other sights.

Of these, by far the most melancholy interest is awakened by the relics of those brave firemen who have died, or have been seriously injured, on duty. In a cupboard, in a long, rather low apartment, in the square or inner quadrangle of the building, are a number of helmets; bruised, battered, broken, burnt ; the fragments of crests twisted by fire, dulled by water and dust and smoke. Here is a saddening record indeed. The visitor experiences much the same sensations as those with which he gazes at the bodies at the Great Saint Bernard, only in this instance the cause of death is fire and heat, in the other snow and vapour, wind and storm ; but all "fulfilling His word," Whose fiat has gone forth, "To dust shalt thou return."

Aye, it is a sad moment when on a canvas

and descend. He was terribly burned. But Jacobs being a stout man—his portrait is hanging on the wall in the office waiting-room in Southwark—could not squeeze through, and he was burned to a cinder, almost. What remained of him was laid to rest with all Brigade honours, but in this museum are his blackened tunic-front, his hatchet and spanner, the nozzle of the hose he held in his death-grip. That is all! But his memory is green, and not a man who mentions but points with pride to his picture. "Did you tell him about Jacobs ?" is a question which testifies to the estimation in which this brave man is held ; and he is but a sample of the rest.

For he is not alone represented. Take the helmets one by one at random. Whose was this ? JOSEPH FORD'S ? Yes, read on, and you will learn that he saved six lives at a fire in Gray's Inn-road, and that he was in the act of saving a seventh when he lost his life. Poor fellow !

Stanley Guernsey; T. Ashford; Hoad; Berg, too, the hero of the Alhambra fire in 1882. But the record is too long. *Requiescant in pace.* They have done their duty; some have survived to do it again, and we may be satisfied. . . . Come away, lock the cupboard, good Number 109. May it be long ere thy helmet is placed with sad memento within this press.

Descending the stairs we reach the office once again. Here we meet our Superintendent. All is quiet. Some men are reading, others writing reports, mayhap; a few are in their shirt-sleeves working, polishing the reserve engine: a calm reigns. We glance up at the automatic fire-alarm which, when just heated, rings the call, and "it will warm up also with your hand." See? Yes! but suppose it should ring, suppose—

Ting, ting, ting, ting-g-g-g!

What's this? The call? I am at the office door in a second. Well it is that I proceed no farther. As I pause in doubt and surprise, the heavy rear doors swing open by themselves as boldly and almost as noiselessly as the iron gate which opened for St. Peter. A clattering of hoofs, a running to and fro for a couple of seconds; four horses trot in, led by the coachman; in the twinkling of an eye the animals are hitched to the ready engines; the firemen dressed, helmeted, and booted are seated on the machines; a momentary pause to learn

at the traces; the passers-by scatter helter-skelter as the horses plunge into the street and then dash round the corner to their stables once again.

"A false alarm?"

"Yes, sir. We thought you'd like to see a turn out, and that is how it's done!"

A false alarm! Was it true? Yes, the men are good-temperedly doffing boots and helmets, and quietly resuming their late avocations. They do not mind. Less than twenty seconds have elapsed, and from a quiet hall the engine-room has been transformed into a bustling fire station. Men, horses, engines all ready and away! No one knew whither he was going. The call was sufficient for all of them. No questions put save one, "Where is it?" Thither the brave fellows would have hurried, ready to do and die, if necessary.

It is almost impossible to describe the effect which this sudden transformation scene produces; the change is so rapid, the effect is so dramatic, so novel to a stranger. We hear of the engines turning out, but to the writer, who was not in the secret, the result was most exciting, and the remembrance will be lasting. The wily artist had placed himself outside, and secured a view, an instantaneous picture of the start; but the writer was in the dark, and taken by surprise. The wonderful rapidity, order, discipline, and exactness of the parts secure a most effective tableau.

A TURN OUT.

their destination ere the coachman pulls the ropes suspended over head; the street doors fold back, automatically, the prancing, rearing steeds impatient, foaming, strain

After such an experience one naturally desires to see the mainspring of all this machinery, the hub round which the wheel revolves—Captain Eyre M. Shaw, C.B.

But the chief officer has slipped out, leaving us permission to interview his empty chair, and the apartments which he daily occupies when on duty in Southwark.

This unpretending room upstairs is plainly but comfortably furnished—though no carpet covers the floor, oilcloth being cooler. Business is writ large on every side. On one wall is a large map of the fire stations of the immense area presided over by Captain Shaw. Here are separately indicated the floating engines, the escapes, ladders, call points, police stations, and private communications.

The chair which "the Captain" has temporarily vacated bristles with speaking tubes. On the walls beside the fire-place are portraits of men who have died on duty ; the chimney-piece is decorated with nozzles — hose-nozzles—of various sizes. Upon the table are reports, map of Paris, and many documents, amid which a novel shines, as indicating touch with the outside world. There is a book-case full of carefully arranged pamphlets, and on the opposite wall an illuminated address of thanks from the Fire Brigade Association to Captain Shaw, which concludes with the expression of a hope "That his useful life may long be spared to fill the high position in the service he now adorns."

With this we cordially concur, and we echo the "heartfelt wishes" of his obliged and faithful servants as we retire, secure in our possession of a picture of the apartment.

There are many interesting items in connection with the Brigade which we find time to chronicle. For instance, we learn that the busiest time is, as one would expect, between September and December. The calls during the year 1889 amounted to 3,131. Of these 594 were false alarms, 199 were only chimneys on fire, and of the remainder 153 only resulted in serious damage, 2,185 in slight damage. These calls are exclusive of ordinary chimney

fires and small cases, but in all those above referred to engines and men were turned out. The grand total of fires amounted to 4,705, or on an average 13 fires, or supposed fires, a day. This is an increase of 350 on those of 1888, and we find that the increment has been growing for a decade. However, considering the increase in the number of houses, there is no cause for alarm. Lives were lost at thirty-eight fires in 1889.

The *personnel* of the Brigade consists of only seven hundred and seven of all ranks. The men keep watches of twelve hours, and do an immense amount of work besides. This force has the control of 158 engines, steam and manual of all sorts ; $31\frac{1}{2}$ miles of hose, and 80

THE REPAIRING SHOP.

carts to carry it ; besides fire-floats, steam tugs, barges, and escapes ; long ladders, trolleys, vans, and 131 horses. These are to attend to 365 call points, 72 telephones to stations, 55 alarm circuits, besides telephones to police stations and public and private building and houses, and the pay is 3s. 6d. per day, increasing !

From these, not altogether dry, bones of facts we may build up a monument to the great energy and intense *esprit de corps* of Captain Shaw and his Brigade. In their hands we place ourselves every night. While the Metropolis sleeps the untiring Brigade watches over its safety. Whether at the head-quarters or at the outer stations, at the street stations, boxes, or escape stations, the men are continually vigilant ; and are most efficiently seconded by the police.

But for the latter force the efforts of the firemen would often be crippled, and their heroic attempts perhaps rendered fruitless, by the pressure of the excited spectators.

We have now seen the manner in which the Metropolitan Fire Brigade is managed, and how it works ; the splendid services it accomplishes, for which few rewards are forthcoming. It is true that a man may attain to the post of superintendent, and to a house, with a salary of £245 a year, but he has to serve a long probation. For consider that he has to learn his drill and the general working of the Brigade. Every man must be competent to perform all the duties. During this course of instruction he is not permitted to attend a fire ; such experience being found unsuitable to beginners. In a couple of months, if he has been a sailor, the recruit is fit to go out, and he is sent to some station, where, as fireman of the fourth class, he performs the duties required.

By degrees, from death or accident, or other causes, those above him are removed, or promoted, and he ascends the ladder to the first class, where, having passed an ex-amination, he gets a temporary appointment as assistant officer on probation. If then satisfactory, he is confirmed in his position as officer, proceeds to head-quarters, and superintends a section of the establishment as inspector of the shops, and finally as drill instructor.

After this service, he is probably put under the superintendent at a station as " engineer-in-charge," as he is termed. He has, naturally, every detail of drill and " business " at his fingers' ends. The wisdom of such an arrangement is manifest. As the engineer-in-charge has been lately through the work of drill instructor, he knows exactly what is to be done, and every other officer in similar position also knows it. Thus uniformity of practice is insured.

There are many other points on which information is most courteously given at head-quarters. But time presses. We accordingly take leave of our pleasant guide, and the most polite of superintendents, and, crossing the Iron Bridge once more, plunge into the teeming thoroughfares of the City, satisfied.

CAPTAIN SHAW'S SANCTUM.

Street Musicians.

By Gilbert Guerdon.

MUSIC "hath charms to soothe," we admit, but not all music, and not at all times ; and it is this modification of the soothing effects of music that our street minstrels, both vocal and instrumental, seem to be unable, or unwilling, to comprehend.

Yet the street minstrelsy of to-day is nothing like so outrageously annoying and worrying as it was twenty years ago. Occasionally only do we hear one of those wretched old barrel-organs which helped to drive Parliament to pass the Act of 1863. That enactment was intended to minimise, or, at least, to modify, the annoyance caused by the so-called music of the streets, and it has succeeded. Speaking generally, there are two kinds of street musicians—the tolerable and the intolerable. Amongst the former, we may include the poor fiddler who tells us that when he is "on the job," he manages to scrape together a decent livelihood. After ten years he has become weather hardened, and his long-tailed frock coat serves for winter or summer, with the only variation of being buttoned or unbuttoned. He has his regular patrons, who look out for him about once a week. One old spinster, who lives in a suburban villa, is always "good for a bob" when he plays "I dreamt that I dwelt in marble halls." Now and then you may hear the old girl warbling out the ballad with the window wide open, much to the amusement of the passers-by. A few doors off lives an old sea captain, whose grandson has always to dance a hornpipe when the fiddler comes round, and the old salt immediately sends out hot rum and water, whatever the time of year.

When the fiddler tries a new locality, he begins with, "The Heart Bowed Down," which scarcely ever fails to bring a sympathetic someone to the window. His average daily takings are from four to five shillings. In the autumn he plays himself down to Margate, and gets a mouthful of fresh air, and plenty of "recognition."

It was an accident that made him take to the tin whistle, or the "American flageolet," as he calls it. Bad luck had compelled him to pawn his fiddle, and, till he could raise the money to get it out again, he had recourse to the cheapest instrument he could think of, and that was the penny tin whistle. He certainly does get some capital tone out of it, and, at a distance, it may be mistaken for the piccolo. He did not, however, make much of his playing till he had the whistle soldered on to a tin coffee-pot, in place of the spout. This took immensely, and the coffee-pot brought in more pence than the fiddle, sometimes as much as eight or nine shillings a day.

Another penny whistler is a blind man, who morning, noon, and night tootles out "The Last Rose of Summer," alternated with a doleful hymn tune. What little money the poor fellow gets is given more out of compassion for his affliction than for any pleasure that his music affords.

Conscious perhaps that his bag-pipes

"THE LAST ROSE OF SUMMER."

alone would not bring in the bawbees, Sandy MacTosh adds the attraction of a Scotch reel or pipe-dance. Dressed in full Highland costume, a little bit frowsy, the piper and his boy march along the

"KILLIM KALLAM."

quiet suburban roads, playing the pipes to attract attention, and stopping at a convenient spot to give the dance. He gets very little encouragement, however, except from his own country people ; but he has found out their homes, and to them he pays regular visits. There is one real old Mac who invariably celebrates his birthday with a feast of haggis and shepherd's pie, and Sandy MacTosh always attends with his pipes to "play in" the haggis. What is a haggis without the accompaniment of a Highland skreel? As food and music, the pudding and the pipes match each other admirably, and by the time the feast is finished, and the Athol Brose has been tipped off, both Mac and the piper are equally ready to sing, "We are na fou'." But for the Highland families— the Lowlanders do not like the pipes—Sandy MacTosh and his tribe would starve. There are in London, perhaps, half a dozen other Highland bag-pipers and a few frauds :—

> "These are Mile-enders,
> Dressed up as Highlanders,
> Shiv'ring in kilts."

For the "Killim Kallam" two long "church warden" pipes are used instead of the crossed swords. The dancing is just as difficult over the clays as over the claymores, and there is no danger of cutting the toes. Saturday night is the most profitable, then Monday, and Friday is the least. Pipers do not often get molested, except by tipsy men, who always want to dance ; but Sandy then turns on the dreary-sounding drone and plays a doleful tune in extra slow time, so the drunken toper has to do an English instead of a Scotch reel.

The Italian tribe of street musicians may be dealt with as a group. There are the bag-pipers, the children with the accordion and triangle, the organ-man and the monkey, and the hurdy-gurdy grinder, all of whom hail from the neighbourhood of Clerkenwell, where there is an Italian colony. At the far

ITALIAN BAGPIPES.

F

"ACCORDION AND TRIANGLE."

end of Leather-lane, in Little Bath-street and Warner-street, they swarm, and there is quite the look and smell and noise of the back slums of an Italian city. The butchers' shops are stocked with the heads, trotters, and "innards" of bullocks, calves, sheep, and pigs, and there is the "Piggy-Wiggy pork-shop," and Italian barbers and cobblers. The Restaurant Italiano Milard is where many of the Italians spend their lazy day—which is Friday. There are also ice-cream makers, roast chestnut "merchants," and dealers in old clothes. Round the latter the Italian women congregate, and bargain for, and try on the gaudy-coloured garments—gowns, petticoats, and shawls; which must have been specially selected to suit the tastes of the Italians.

At the corner of Little Bath-street is the headquarters of the organ-grinders. There they congregate early in the morning before they start on their rounds, and distribute their monkeys, babies,

and dancing children. The premises belong to one of the principal makers of piano-organs in London, and the whole of the ground floor is arranged as a depôt, where some hundreds of instruments are stored. Part of them may be hired, but most of them are owned by the people we see playing them in the streets. A small sum is charged for "shed room," and any alterations or repairs can be done on the premises. The proprietors are Italians, and are spoken of as very fair-dealing people. We found, on inquiry, that at least half of the owners of the piano-organs are English people, who have bought their instruments, paying £10 or £15 for them by instalments. The charge for hire is about 10s. per week. There is a choice of all the latest popular operatic and music-hall tunes, and generally all the tunes are changed every six months, though some tunes, like "The Lost Chord" and "The Village Blacksmith," are seldom taken off the barrels. A piano-organ, if taken care of and protected from the wet, will last ten or twelve years. A new tune, if not very florid, can be put in for 9s. or 10s.

The monkey organ-man with the old-fashioned discordant barrel-organ is an old stager—the original "organ-grinder." He looks out for the streets where straw is laid down, and begins to grind directly. An

"THE MONKEY ORGAN-MAN."

enraged *pater-familias*, who has just carefully tied up the knocker with a white kid glove, and muffled all the bells, calls out to the man, "Go away, do. Don't you see the straw?" The organ-grinder touches his hat, grins, sends the monkey to climb up the water-pipe, and begins another tune. Ultimately he gets locked up, and then coolly tells the magistrate that he did not go away because he thought the straw was put down so that the noise of the carts should not drown the music!

"HURDY-GURDY."

The Savoyard hurdy-gurdy player is almost extinct. The music is produced by the friction of a wheel on one or more strings, and the tone is regulated by pressure on keys. The men admit that they get more money for sitting as artists' models than from playing. The hurdy-gurdy is amongst stringed instruments what the bag-pipes are amongst the wind instruments, but yet no one ever hears them played together. Probably the players themselves could not stand the combined noise.

The Italians send out their wives with two babies—not always their own — and, when the children get big enough, they take the place of the almost obsolete monkey, and do the begging. Older Italian girls pick up a lot of money in the City, and their success has prompted several

English and Irish girls to imitate them by colouring their skins with walnut juice, and rigging themselves out in the Italian style. Many of these girls in earlier life danced round the piano-organs in the streets, and were paid to do so by the organ-grinders, as people who would give nothing for the music would give a penny to see the little ones dancing. Such a juvenile "*Bal al fresco*" makes a pretty picture, not thought unworthy of the walls of the Royal Academy.

Amongst the intolerable street musicians must certainly be placed the Indian tom-tom player. His instrument is a drum of a very primitive kind, made out of a section of the hollow trunk of a tree, over each end of which a skin is tightly stretched. It is about the size of an oyster barrel, and the noise is produced by beating it with the hands. There are but two tones—one from each end—and the mournful monotony of the

"OUT WITH THE BABIES."

"A 'BAL AL FRESCO.'"

orchestra at a theatre, and now picks up a pretty penny by playing in the evening in the West-end squares. He don't care for permanent engagements, and prefers to be "on his own hook," though he occasionally chums up with another street musician— Old Blowhard, who plays the cornet-à-piston. He only plays by ear, and can, therefore, only manage a few tunes, to which the bassoonist extemporises a telling bass. According to the bassoonist, "Blowhard is a rattling old boy when in a good humour, but he's awful short-tempered; and often when in the middle of a duet— especially in 'All's Well'—he'll stop blowing, call me nasty names, and step it. But he soon comes round again, and soaps me over by playing very feelingly—

> 'I love new friends, but still give me
> The dear, dear friends of old.'"

According to Blowhard, "Pumper"—that is, the bassoonist—is all right when he plays fair, but he *will* put in flourishes and fireworks, which puts me out and spoils everything."

music is only varied by a few notes of a tuneless song which the player now and then puts in. The servant girls are his principal patrons, and some years since

"TOM-TOM."

one of these tom-tomers completely captivated a young English cook-maid and married her.

The bassoonist admits that he has seen better days, but he enjoys playing his awkward-looking instrument, and, when in the humour, plays it remarkably well. He was once in a military band, then in an

"THE BASSOONIST."

"OLD BLOWHARD."

as it does, of glass tumblers sufficient in number to represent about two octaves of notes. They are arranged on a light table in two rows, like a harmonicon. The pitch of the notes is regulated by the quantity of water put into each tumbler. One glass is reserved for lemon-juice and water, into which the performer now and then dips his fingers. The sound is produced by rubbing the wet fingers on the

MUSICAL GLASSES.

Perhaps the oldest and least objection-able of the street musicians is the campano-logist, or, as he styles himself, "The Royal Bell-Ringer." He makes a pitch in a quiet street or alley, and rigs up his ten bells on a tightened wire. With a short stick in each hand, he strikes his bells, and pro-duces some pleasing melodies : the general favourites are "Home, Sweet Home" and "The Blue Bells of Scotland"; and he generally concludes with a wedding peal.

Scarcely anyone can object to the per-former on the musical glasses. His "instrument" is simple enough, consisting,

"THE ROYAL BELL-RINGER."

rim of the glasses, and some very pleasing music is the result. Ac-cording to your nationality you can have "Home, Sweet Home," "Ye Banks and Braes," "My Name's Edward Morgan," or "The Banks of Allan Water."

The "One Man Band" is a well-known character. He began life with a Punch and Judy show, and then played the drum and pan-pipes.

The ballad singer seldom starts on his rounds before dusk, and he is careful to get a report whispered widely about that he is the "deputy leading tenor of the London Opera Company, and don't want to be seen by daylight, as it might injure his reputation." He is above being questioned, and tells you bluntly, "If you've got anything for the shell, why, shell out; if not, shut up. I'll sing you your favourite song, but there's no time for gabbing." He has a powerful and fairly good voice, and knows how to use it. He occasionally says he has a cold and then he puts in an execrable deputy, which further exalts his own powers and himself in the opinion of his admirers. He sings the latest and most popular songs, and evidently pockets plenty of money, especially in the autumn at seaside places like Margate and Ramsgate.

"ONE MAN BAND."

Being of an inventive turn of mind he added to his instruments the tambourine, triangle, and cymbals, which he played by leg movements. Then he added a concertina strapped to the left arm, a pair of clappers occupied his left hand, and with his right hand he played a hurdy-gurdy. The cap and jingling bells on his head completed "the band." All these instruments were carefully kept in tune with each other, and the performer produced some passable dance music of the country-fair type, while his boy took round the collecting shell. There are several similar performers about the country, but none with so many instruments.

"BALLAD SINGER."

"WACHT-AM-RHEIN."

Our German friends, who have so considerately left their "Happy Fatherland" to test the English taste for music, are happily getting less numerous every year, but there are still a few left —some tolerable, some otherwise. They are brought over from the agricultural parts of Germany by an enterprising bandmaster, who gives them four shillings a week, pays their fares, provides instruments, uniforms, board and lodging, and teaches them to play some instrument. Their pay increases according to the progress they make. Fulham is their headquarters and Sunday their practice day. The novices begin playing in the northern and eastern suburbs of London, and, as they improve, they are promoted to the south-west and west. A guide goes with them, and he does the collecting. Denmark Hill being a favourite residential locality for well-to-do Germans the best bands generally work—or rather play—that way.

"PETTICOAT QUARTETTE."

Dogs, especially singing dogs, take great delight in German bands, and may often be seen, with their noses skyward, lifting up their voices in grand chorus, and are no doubt supremely disgusted that their efforts to increase the harmony are not appreciated by the bandsmen.

The Petticoat Quartette comprises four girls, supposed to be sisters. But they are none of them communicative, and the answer of the eldest one to our first question was somewhat startling: " Ask my Pa," said the lady, to the innocent question, " Are you all sisters ? " Where they picked up their playing powers, what they earn, and other cognate inquiries were answered by the equivalent of " What's that to you ? " They appear to have been pestered a good deal with proposals from trousered street musicians, to join their band ; as the eldest said emphatically, " We don't want no perfessional help from no-body." This reply, and an injunction from one of the crowd to " Let the gals alone," checked further inquiries.

With regard to the " Nigger Minstrels " there is nothing new to be said, and it has not yet been discovered why the singing of men with blackened hands and faces is liked, when the singing and playing of the same men with uncoloured skins would not be tolerated. Niggers—real niggers—never could either sing or play, but our " Nigger Minstrels " can do both.

Some street musicians at this time of the year—happily only a few—make a little overtime as waits, and keep us in mind of " The Mistletoe Bough."

At the Animals' Hospital.

A HAPPY FAMILY IN BONE.

NE hundred years ago! A century since the first two stones were joined together from which was to spring a veritable boon to the sick and suffering amongst all sorts and conditions of domesticated animals— an abiding-place where horse and dog, calf and sheep, even down to the maligned and sorely-tried drawer of the costermonger's cart might receive assistance and advice to meet the thousand and one ills to which their flesh and bones are heir. The Royal Veterinary College is within a month of claiming a hundred years' good labour to its credit.

Hence the reason of our mounting the "knife-board" of a yellow-bodied 'bus, conspicuously painted "Camden Town," with a view of obtaining a preliminary interview with the driver regarding the ills of most animals in general, and of horse-flesh in particular. He knew little, and kept that meagre knowledge to himself, regarding us with suspicion, probably as a spy in the employ of an opposition company, and screwed his mouth artfully when a question was volleyed, and met it with a

knowing crack of the whip in irritating response.

"Orf side down, 'Arry. Just show the way where the donkeys is doctored, and the 'osses waccinated. Whoa! Whoa! 'Er', 'pon my word, 'Arry, if I didn't forget to give Betsy"—a frisky-looking mare on the near side—"her cough mixture. Wot time does the Wet'inary College shut?"

The way pointed out by the conductor was King-street, at the top of which runs Great College-street, where the great gates of the Hospital for Animals are facing you. Here, congregated together about the entrance, are a dozen or twenty students, the majority of them arrayed in garments of a decidedly "horsey" cut, their appearance suggesting that they are somewhere about one remove from the medical student proper, though in full possession of all their traditional love of fun and irrepressible spirits. For a charge of sixty guineas these young men may revel in the anatomy of a horse for a period of three years, walk the straw-carpeted floor of the sick stable, pay periodical visits, and learn how to prescribe the necessary remedies for the inmates of the dogs' ward. The secretary, Mr. R.

A. N. Powys, assures us that three hundred students are at present located here, and, together with the educational staff, numbering, amongst others, such veterinary authorities as Professors Axe, Penberthy, McQueen, Coghill, and Edwards, they visit the beds of some fifty horses

THE RESULTS OF SWALLOWING TIN-TACKS.

every day, together with those of some ten or a dozen dogs, to say nothing of pigs and sheep weakly inclined, and cows of nervous temperament. During the past twelve months 1,174 horses have been examined for unsoundness. More than four thousand animals were treated either as in-patients or out-patients during that period.

Passing through the gateway, a fine open space is immediately in front, with a roadway laid down for the purpose of testing the soundness of horses. Just at this moment a fine prancing steed, a typical shire horse, with his coat as brown as a new chestnut, and his limbs and quarters as they should be, is led out by a stalwart groom. For all the animal's 16½ hands, there is a question as to his soundness. A professor hurries up, followed by a score of students, with note-books and pencils ready. The horse is trotted round the gravel-path, then galloped with a rider bare-back. A thoughtful consultation follows, and the verdict pronounced upon its respiratory organs is: "As sound as a bell."

There is an estimable and enterprising gentleman touring the London streets who is the proprietor of a group of animals which he facetiously calls "The Happy Family." These are in the flesh, alive and frolicsome; but here in Camden Town, where all things veterinary are studied, is a happy family—in the bone. They are gathered together in unison around the bust of the late Professor Robertson. The "ship of the desert" has on its left an elephant of formidable size, near which stands an ostrich. On the camel's right is a cow, and a lion, originally part of a menagerie

in the Edgware-road. A pig is readily recognised, and a fine dog seems to be looking up to the late Professor as an old friend. This interesting collection will shortly be added to by all that is left of the celebrated race-horse "Hermit."

It is to the Museum that the students repair two or three times a week, and gain a practical knowledge of the ailments which are associated with animals.

The glass cases contain horses' mouths, showing the various stages of the teeth. Innumerable are the bottles holding preserved portions of each and every animal. In one of the cases is a very interesting specimen of the students' work. It illustrates the anatomy of a dog's leg. The bone is taken in hand by the student, and by an ingenious arrangement of red sealing wax the blood-vessels are faithfully and realistically introduced.

Every case contains a curiosity—one is full of the feet of horses, and its next-door neighbour protects a wonderful array of horseshoes. The ideal horse-shoe is one which requires no nails. The nearest approach to this is a shoe which clamps the hoof, is screwed up tightly, and the whole thing kept in place by an iron band. The great amount of pressure which is required to keep the shoe from shifting, and the possible injury it may cause the wearer, has prevented its universal use.

Here is an old-fashioned drenching bit— the old idea of administering medicine to horses. The bit is hollow and a funnel is attached to it, to be inserted in the animal's mouth and the mixture poured in. To-day, however, a tin drenching can of a somewhat pyramidical shape is simply used.

At the door one may brush against what appears to be a mop of extra size. It is—to use a homely expression—a calf's leg with "a housemaid's knee." This curious growth is five feet in circumference and a foot and a half in

"POLLY."

depth. But perhaps the most remarkable corner is that devoted to the storing of massive stones and cement, hardened together, which have been taken from the bodies of various animals.

These are of all shapes and sizes. Two of them taken from a mare, weigh fifty-four pounds, and many of them would turn the

employed in lameness, as a blister on the limb. It is interesting to be told that there are a number of horses in the hunting field, in the streets, and the park, wearing silver tracheotomy tubes, as an assistance to their breathing, and, to put it in the words of a doctor, "doing well."

The pharmacy is by no means to be

" JOE."

scale at thirty-five to forty pounds. The formation of such stones is curious. Above is a drawing—in miniature—of a huge stone formed inside a cow. The cow—by no means a careful one—enjoyed the green grass of the meadow in blissful ignorance that even tin-tacks and nails get lodged on the sward occasionally. The cow, in her innocence, swallowed the nail—there it is, imbedded in the centre. Lime and earth deposited and hardened round it, with the result that an immense stone was formed of nearly forty pounds in weight.

Next comes the instrument room. This is an apartment not calculated to act as a sedative upon the visitor who is forced to be a frequent caller on the dentist. The forceps for drawing horses' teeth are more than a yard long, and it requires a man of might and muscle to use them with effect. The tracheotomy tubes—inserted when a horse has difficulty in breathing—stand out brightly from amongst the dull and heavy appearance of the firing irons, which are

hurriedly passed by. It is the chemist's shop of the establishment, the place where students enter to be initiated into all the mysteries of compounding a prescription. They may crush the crystals into powder in a mortar of diminutive size, or pound them in one as big as a copper with a pestle as long as a barber's pole. A great slate is covered with veterinary hieroglyphics; the shelves are decorated with hundreds of blue bottles, the drawers brimming over with tiny phials and enormous gallipots. Step behind a substantial wooden screen, which practically says " Private," and you have the most approved of patterns in the way of a chemist's counter. Here is every item, down to the little brass scales and weights, the corks and sealing wax, the paper and string.

From the pharmacy to the Turkish bath is but a step. Veterinary authorities have arrived at the conclusion that a Turkish bath is the finest remedy that can be found for skin disease in horses. This takes the form of a square stable, heated by a furnace at the back. Not an outlet is permitted for the escape of the hot air, and it can be heated to any temperature required. The horse, too, can enjoy all the luxuriousness of a shower bath, and if necessary can dabble his four feet in a foot-bath handy. Indeed, everything goes to prove the whole system of treating sick animals is founded on the same principle as that meted out to human beings.

One must needs look in at the open door of the shoeing-forge. The clang of the blacksmith's hammer makes a merry accompaniment to the prancing of a dozen fine creatures just entering to be shod. The whistling of the bellows, and the hissing of the roused-up flames vie with the snorting of a grand bay mare who cannot be numbered amongst the most patient of her sex.

"Stand over, miss—stand over," cries a strapping, brawny lad. "She'll take a number five;" and from a stock of three hundred and fifty dozen new shoes which adorn the walls—and, if numbers count for anything, good luck should pervade every nook and corner of the forge—a five-inch shoe is quickly adjusted, and the bay, not yet realising the new footing upon which she stands, enlists the services of a pair of men to hold her in.

The paddock in the immediate neighbourhood of the forge is the sick-ward of the hospital for horses. Every horse has its own apartment—a loose box, the door of which is fitted with iron bars through which the doctor can inspect his patient. The inmate's card, which tells its sex and colour, date of entrance, number, disease, and treatment prescribed, is affixed to the door, and every day a professor goes his rounds. The hospital surgeon also pays continual visits, and medicine is administered at intervals varying from two or three hours to three or four days.

Here is one of the most patient of the inmates, "Polly," a pretty creature who would add to the picturesqueness of any hunting-field in the country, and who has dislocated her shoulder. Polly might be held up as a credit to any hospital. She bore her bandaging—not always a painless operation, for the linen must needs be fastened firmly —without moving a muscle, only heaving a sigh of relief as soon as the tying-up was over.

A slip of linen or calico is carefully cut to size and strapped on with strong tapes. It is likewise considered beneficial that the patient should be kept in ignorance as to its whereabouts: for the horror of "hospital" which pervades most people's minds exists in the imaginations of animals as well. Therefore the sick Polly must needs submit to having her eyes bandaged that she may realise the position of being in the dark as to her lodging for a week or two. A strip of the same material from which the shoulder-strap was cut is tied on to the head-collar.

"Polly's" next-door neighbour, however, presents a much more serious case.

"Joe" has recently been gaining experience in the fact that life is but a chapter of accidents. Joe could not be characterised as a careless creature ; indeed, it is chronicled of him that he would positively feel for every step he took, and pick out the safest spots in the line of route. Poor Joe ! His careful line of action and method of travelling did not meet with that reward to which it was entitled. Alas ! he now rests here as a warning to his fellow-horses not to put trust in the treacherous smoothness of the agreeable asphalt, or too much faith in the comfort afforded by the pleasures of travelling on a newly-repaired road. He is laid up with an in-

" DAVID."

jured thigh, and a severe fracture has befallen one half of what he depended upon to carry him through life.

" Rest, complete rest, is what he needs," remarks a passing doctor. And a very ingenious arrangement is provided in order to attain the desired end.

This consists of a big canvas sling, held up by half a dozen pulleys. On this the whole weight of the body is supported, and the comfort afforded is equivalent to that provided by a good bed to a weary man. The animal is so weak that, if he tumbled down, it is doubtful whether he would get up again. Here he will remain until completely recovered, which means enjoying the repose afforded by this horsey hammock for a period between six weeks and six months.

The two fractured limbs are, for the time being, imbedded in iron splints with leather bands, and fitted with little pads in front in order not to cut the leg. All these surgical appliances are in every way as perfect as if they were intended for the human frame, instead of for a horse's.

Sickness does not seem to diminish the appetites of the inmates, and doses of iron and quinine are not of frequent occurrence. It may take three or four months to cure a case of lameness, and long terms of confinement may possibly be needed for diseases of the respiratory or digestive organs, or of the skin. But the bill for food, hay and straw, amounted to the comfortable sum of £1,510 0s. 8d. last year, against the modest outlay of £166 11s. 5d. which was spent in drugs. The number of horse-patients confined to well-kept beds of straw and healthy peat-moss, in admirably ventilated apartments, averages fifty at one time. Their paddock—or sick-ward—is a pattern of cleanliness, neatness, and good order.

There is only a moment to spend in the operating theatre, acknowledged to be the finest in Europe. It is a huge space covered with a glass canopy, where four or five horses can be operated on at once. There is ample accommodation for every student in the hospital to obtain a good view of the proceedings. Only a moment also to peep in at a little apartment in the far

corner—a small operating room fitted up with a trevis, a wooden structure where the animal to be operated upon is placed, and strapped in with ropes, so that movement

THE NURSERY.

is impossible ; only a moment, such a barking and a whining breaks upon the peaceful air—troublous cries that find an outlet from the open door of an upper room, to which ascends a stable staircase. It is the dogs' ward !

The barking of the inmates is to be interpreted into an unmistakable welcome. Here, in corners of the cosiest, and beds of the whitest wood-fibre, reclines many a magnificent specimen. These fine St. Bernard pups are worth £250 a piece, and only a week or two ago a patient was discharged as convalescent, upon whose head rested the figure of £1,200. Most of them are suffering from skin disease ; but here is a pup, with a coat of impenetrable blackness, afflicted with St. Vitus's dance. He wears a pitiful expression ; but, save for an occasional twitter of a muscle, rests very quietly. Every cage is occupied, save one, and that is an apartment with double iron gates. It is set apart for mad dogs. Every creature bears its affliction with remarkable resignation, and, as one passes from bed to bed, runs out to the length of its chain and stands looking up the sawdust-strewn floor which leads to "the nursery."

One fine fellow, however, rests in a

corner, near the bath, the very personification of all that is dignified.

"David" is a grand St. Bernard, upon whom a coat of shaggy beauty has been

the iron bars, and his leg was broken. The child was quite safe ; she was only gathering flowers.

"The Nursery" is a room set apart a

DISSECTING ROOM.

bestowed and the blessing of a majestic presence. He sits there with his front paw dangling over the bed-side ; helpless, but not uncared for. His leg is broken, and he holds it out, tightly tied up and bandaged, as token thereof. Cheer up, David, old boy— look a bit pleasant, David, my brave fellow. But David only shakes his head in grateful thanks for a word of sympathy. He is a credit to his breed, and his noble disposition would lead him to forget what brought him there. It is a touching story. His owner's little daughter was his mistress ; David followed her wherever she went, and—save at night time—never allowed her out of his sight, and even then he would nestle outside her door on the mat, until the child woke in the morning. Just a week ago the little girl had wandered down the river bank, climbing over the iron railings separating the pathway from the tiny valley which led down to the water. David did not notice this action, and when he turned his head saw that his mistress had disappeared. With his mind bent on the water, he took a leap, intending to spring over the rails ; but his front paw caught

the far end for the reception of the smaller species of the canine tribe.

The two little Skye terriers fondling one another are suffering from ingrown toe-nails and must needs have them cut. The cot next to them is empty ; but a "King Charles" will convert the apartment into a royal one on the morrow. His Majesty, too, requires the application of the scissors to his royal toes. Above is a terrier— beautifully marked—but, withal, wearing a remarkably long expression of countenance. Something is wrong with one of his ears, and his face is tied up like that of an individual writhing beneath the tortures of toothache. "Dot" envies his brother terrier next door. There is nothing wrong with *him ;* he is not an inmate, but a boarder, and the property of one of the officials. A pretty little couple of colleys are sympathising with each other in their affliction as they lie cuddled up in the corner. They are both queer—something wrong with their lungs.

Out in the open again, we look in upon a fine bullock with a very ugly swollen face. But here, in a corner all to itself, we meet with a veritable curiosity—a cow with a wooden leg !

This is a strapping young Alderney, of such value that it was deemed advisable to provide her with a wooden support instead of killing her at once. "Susan" was a pet, and had her own way in most things. Probably this aroused the

"SUSAN."

green-eyed monster within the breast of a mare who sometimes shared her meadow. Whether the cause was jealousy or not, one thing is certain—after a particularly hearty meal, which seems to have endowed the mare with exceptional strength and vigour, to say nothing of a wicked and revengeful mind, she deliberately, and without warning, kicked the fair Susan. Susan had to lie up for three or four months, and now a wooden leg supports her injured frame.

A strap is fastened round the body of the cow ; then a wooden support is placed near the neck and attached to the main strap with leather bands. Finally, the iron-bound timber leg is set in place ; and it is said that the animal sustains but little inconvenience.

Following a number of students, we are soon within the precincts of the dissecting room. This is a square room containing a dozen or twenty dead donkeys, each laid out on a table for dissection. The enterprising students repair to Islington Cattle Market, and for a pound or thirty shillings purchase a likely subject from an obliging coster-monger. Half a dozen of them will each take a share in the expense incurred, and work together at a table, passing from head to tail until a complete examination has been made.

But what most interests the casual visitor is "The Poor Man's Corner," a portion of the yard set apart for out-patients, and termed by the hospital authorities their "cheap practice."

Every day—excepting Sundays—between the hours of two and four, a motley crowd assembles here, bringing with them an animal which has betrayed signs to its owner that it is not altogether "fit." The cabby who is the proud possessor of a four-wheeler and an ancient-looking steed comes with a face which tells another tale than that which be-tokens a small fare. The coster thrusts his hands deep into his trousers pockets and waits in gloomy meditation. Visions of his donkey being condemned to death on the spot flash through his mind, and he almost re-grets he came.

"Guvnor—I say, guvnor, it ain't a 'opeless case, is it ? Don't say it's all up wi' it. Yer see, guvnor, I couldn't help but bring it along. I'm a rough 'un, but I've got a 'art, and, there, I couldn't stand it no longer, seein' the poor creeter a limpin' along like that. On'y say it ain't a 'opeless case."

He will soon be out of his suspense, for his donkey will be examined in its turn.

Not only is advice given gratis and the animal thoroughly examined, but, should it need medicine, or call for an operation, this is readily done, the students generally performing it under the superintendence of one of the professors.

The "poor man's" gate has just been opened, and Mr. E. R. Edwards, the hospital surgeon, holds the bridle of the first horse for examination as the students gather round. One of the professors appears upon the scene, and asks the owner what is the matter with his horse.

"He can 'ardly walk, sir."

"Lame, eh ? "

"I expec's so, sir."

"What are you ? "

"Hawks wegetables about, sir."

The horse is trotted up the yard and back again. Then the professor turns to a student and asks what he considers is wrong with the animal.

"Lame in both hind legs ; "—and, the student having diagnosed the case correctly, the animal is walked off to be further treated and prescribed for.

Case after case is taken. One horse that draws firewood from seven in the morning until ten or eleven at night, cannot eat. Away it goes for examination, and the temperature of its pulse is taken. A lad, evidently not used to the stubborn disposition and immovable spirit of donkeys in general, has brought his own, which he informs the professor he only purchased "the week afore last." Now, nothing under the sun in the shape of argument with whip or words will make it go at anything like the pace which the man from whom he bought it guaranteed.

"Why, sir, I had to drag it here. 'Pon my word, I believe as 'ow he knew where I was a takin' 'im, for he crawled more'n ever. I thought as 'ow there might be something wrong wi' his wind."

"Trot him along," said the professor; but the donkey turned a deaf ear to the inviting cries of forty or fifty students to "go on," and bravely stood his ground. The victor was placed on one side to be dealt with later on.

The next case was one connected with a pathetic story. The horse—a poor creature which had evidently seen better days—was owned by a laundryman, a widower, who had eleven children to support, the oldest of whom was only fifteen years of age, and the youngest six months. He depended entirely on his horse to carry the laundry round from house to house.

The poor fellow stood quietly by and seemed to read in the professor's face and gather from his hurried consultation with a brother "vet." that something out of the common was the matter with his horse. In response to the doctor's beckoning, he approached the spot where the animal stood, and, with tears in his eyes, asked in a choking voice, "Not an operation, I hope, sir?"

The professor shook his head.

Then the truth flashed upon the laundryman's mind. He stood dumbfounded for a moment. The students ceased their chatter, and, save for the movement of a horse's foot upon the uneven stones, the yard was as still as the ward of a hospital where human beings lie. The horse was condemned to death!

The poor fellow threw his arms about the animal's neck, and the horse turned its head in response to his master's caresses, and the cry which came from the man's heart could not have been more pitiful had he been parting from his only friend.

"POOR MAN'S CORNER."

HEADQUARTERS AT WAPPING.

HERE was a time when the owners of craft on the Thames practically left their back-doors open and invited the river-thieves to enter, help themselves, and leave unmolested and content. The barges lay in the river holding everything most coveted, from precious cargoes of silk to comfortable-looking bales of tobacco, protected only from wind, weather, and wicked fingers by a layer of tarpaulin—everything ready and inviting to those who devoted their peculiar talents and irrepressible instincts to the water. Goods to the value of a million sterling were being neatly appropriated every year. The City merchants were at their wits' end. Some of the more courageous and determined of them ventured out themselves at night; but the thieves—never at a loss in conceiving an ingenious and ready means of escape—slipped, so to speak, out of their would-be captors' hands by going semi-clothed about their work, greasing their flesh and garments until they were as difficult to catch as eels.

So the merchants held solemn conclave, the result of which was the formation, in 1792, of "The Preventative Service," a title which clung to the members thereof until 1839, when they were embodied with the Metropolitan Police with the special privilege of posing as City constables. Now they are a body of two hundred and two strong, possessing twenty-eight police galleys and a trio of steam launches. From a million pounds' worth of property stolen yearly a hundred years ago, they have, by a persistent traversing of a watery beat, reduced it to one hundred pounds. Smuggling is in reality played out, though foggy nights are still fascinating to those so inclined ; but now they have to be content with a coil or two of old rope, an ingot of lead, or a few fish. Still the river-policeman's eye and the light of his lantern are

INSPECTOR FLETCHER.

IN THE CELLS.

always searching for suspicious characters and guilty-looking craft.

In High-street, Wapping, famous for its river romances, and within five hundred yards of the Old Stairs, the principal station of the Thames Police is to be found. The traditional blue lamp projects over a somewhat gloomy passage leading down to the river-side landing stage. To us, on the night appointed for our expedition, it is a welcome beacon as to the whereabouts of law and order, for only a few minutes previously half a dozen worthy gentlemen standing at the top of some neighbouring steps, wearing slouched hats and anything but a comforting expression on their faces gruffly demanded, " Do you want a boat ? " Fortunately we did not. These estimable individuals had only just left the dock of the police station, where they had been charged on suspicion, but eventually discharged.

It is a quarter to six o'clock. At six we are to start for our journey up the river as far as Waterloo and back again to Greenwich ; but there is time to take a hasty survey of the interior of the station, where accommodation is provided for sixteen single men, with a library, reading-room, and billiard-room at their disposal.

"Fine night, sir ; rather cold, though," says a hardy-looking fellow dressed in a reefer and a brightly glazed old-time man-o'-war's hat. He is one of the two oldest men in the force, and could tell how he lost his wife and all his family, save one lad, when the *Princess Alice* went down in 1878. He searched for ten days and ten nights, but they were lost to him. Another of these river guardians has a never-to-be-forgotten reminiscence of that terrible disaster, when the men of the Thames police were on duty for four or five nights at a stretch. He was just too late to catch the ill-fated vessel! He was left behind on the pier at Sheerness, and with regret watched it leave, full of merrymakers. What must have been his thoughts when he heard the news?

strapping fellow, buttoning up his coat to his neck.

"Aye, aye, skipper," we shout, becoming for the moment quite nautical.

Inside the station-house you turn sharply to the right, and there is the charge-room. Portraits of Sir Charles Warren and other

A NIGHT CHARGE.

You may pick out any of these thick-set fellows standing about. They have one and all roamed the seas over. Many are old colonials, others middle-aged veterans from the navy and merchant service—every one of them as hard as a rock, capable of rowing for six or eight hours at a stretch without resting on the oar.

"Don't be long inside, sir," shouts a

police authorities are picturesquely arranged on the walls. In front of the desk, with its innumerable little wooden rails, where sits the inspector in charge, is the prisoners' dock, from the ground of which rises the military measurement in inches against which the culprit testifies as to his height. The hands of the clock above are slowly going their rounds. In a corner, near the stout steel rails of the dock, lie a couple of bargemen's peak caps. They are labelled with a half-sheet of notepaper. Their history? They have been picked up in the river, but the poor fellows who owned them are—missing! It will be part of our duties to assist in the search for them to-night.

Just in a crevice by the window are the telegraph instruments. A clicking noise is heard, and the inspector hurriedly takes down on a slate a strange but suggestive message.

"Information received of a prize-fight for £2 a side, supposed to take place between Highgate and Hampstead."

What has Highgate or Hampstead to do with the neighbourhood of Wapping, or how does a prize-fight affect the members of the Thames police, who are anything but pugilistically inclined? In our innocence we learn that it is customary to telegraph such information to all the principal stations throughout London. The steady routine of the force is to be admired.

There are countless coats, capes, and caps hanging in a room through which we

and a drinking cup. Heat is supplied through hot-water pipes ; a pillow and rug are provided for the women ; and, like "desirable villa residences," the apartments are fitted with electric bells.

Here the occupier is lodged for the time being, allowed food at each meal to the value of fourpence, and eventually tried at the Thames Police-court. Look at the doors. They bear countless dents from the boot-tips of young men endeavouring to perform the clever acrobatic feat of kicking out the iron grating over the door through which the gas-jet gives them light. Those of a musical nature ring the electric bell for half an hour at a time, imagining that they are disturbing the peace of the officer in a distant room. But our smart constable, after satisfying himself that all is well, disconnects the current, and sits smiling at his ease. Some of the inmates, too, amuse themselves by manufacturing streamers out of the blankets. They never do it a second time.

Now we are on our way to the riverside.

GOING ON DUTY.

pass on our way to the cells—cosy, clean, and convenient apartments, and decidedly cheap to the temporary tenant. There are two of them, one being specially retained for women. They are painted yellow, provided with a wash-basin, towel, a supply of soap,

We descend the wooden steps, soaked through with the water which only a few hours previously has been washing the stairs. Our boat is in waiting, manned by three sturdy fellows, under the charge of an inspector. It is a glorious night ; the moon seems to have come out just to throw a light upon our artist's note-book, and to provide a picture of the station standing out in strong relief. The carpenter—for they repair their own boats here—looks out from his shop door, and shouts a cheery "Good-

of ingenuity was rewarded with ten years' penal servitude.

Our little craft has a lively time amongst the fire-floats—for fires are just as likely to occur on the river as on the land, and accordingly small launches are dotted about here

POLICE LAUNCH "ALERT."

night." Our galley receives a gentle push into the water, and we start on a long beat of seven and a half miles.

Save for the warning of a passing tug, the river is as a place of the dead. How still and solemn! But a sudden "Yo-ho" from the inspector breaks the quietude.

It is the method of greeting as one police galley passes another.

"Yo-ho!" replies the man in charge of the other boat.

"All right. Good-night."

These river police know every man who has any business on the water at night. If the occupant of a boat was questioned, and his "Yo-ho" did not sound familiar, he would be "towed" to the station.

A simple "Yo-ho" once brought about a smart capture. The rower was mystified at the magic word, got mixed in his replies, and accordingly was accommodated with a private room at the station for the night. It transpired that this river purloiner had stolen the boat, and, being of a communicative disposition, was in the habit of getting on friendly terms with the watchmen of the steamers, and so contrived to gain an entrance to the cabins, from which money and watches disappeared. This piece

and there, fulfilling the same duties as the more formidable - looking engines on *terra firma*. A red light signifies their whereabouts, and they usually lie alongside the piers, so as to be able to telephone quickly should a fire occur. If the police saw flames, they would act exactly as their comrades do on land, and hurry to the nearest float to give the alarm.

It blows cold as we spin past Traitor's Gate at the Tower, but our men become weather-beaten on the Thames, and their hands never lose the grip of the oar. They need a hardy frame, a robust constitution, for no matter what the weather, blinding snow or driving rain, these water guardians come out—the foggiest night detains them not ; they have to get through the fog and their allotted six hours. At the time of the Fenian scare at the House of Correction, thirty-six hours at a stretch was considered nothing out of the way.

Now the lights of Billingsgate shine out, and we experience a good deal of dodging outside the Custom House. The wind is getting up, and the diminutive sprat-boats are taking advantage of the breeze to return home. Some are being towed along. And as the oars of our little craft touch the water, every man's eyes are fixed in order to catch sight of anything like the appearance of a missing person. A record of the missing, as well as the found, is kept at the station we have just left a mile or two down the river. Ten poor creatures remain yet to be discovered. What stories, thrilling and heartrending, we have to listen to! Yet even in such pitiful occurrences as these, much that is grimly humorous often surrounds them. Many are the sad recognitions on the part of those "found drowned." Experience has taught the police to stand quietly behind those who must needs go through such a terrible ordeal, and who often swoon at the first sight. Where is a more touching story than that of the little girl who tramped all the way from Camden Town to Wapping, for the purpose of identifying her father, who had been picked up near the Old Stairs? She was a brave little lass, and looked up into the policeman's face as he took her by the hand and walked with her towards the mortuary. As they reached the door and opened it, the bravery of the child went to the man's heart. He was used to this sort of thing, but, when he thought of the orphan, the tears came to his eyes; he turned away for a moment, lest his charge should see them and lose what strength her tiny frame possessed. He hesitated before he let her go in.

"You're not frightened, are you, policeman?" she asked innocently.

He could not move, and she went in alone. When the constable followed, he found the child with her arms round her dead father's neck, covering his face with tears and kisses.

We shoot beneath London Bridge, and the commotion brought about by a passing tug causes our men to rest their oars as we are lifted like a cork by the disturbed waves. And as the great dome of St. Paul's appears in sight, standing out solemnly against the black night, we pull our wraps around us, as a little preliminary to a story volunteered by the captain of our crew. The river

police could tell of many a remarkable clue to identification—a piece of lace, or the button of a man's trousers. But the inspector has a curious story of a watch to relate—true every word of it.

"Easy!" he cries to his men—"look to it—now get along," and to the steady swing of the oars he commences.

"It all turned on the inscription engraved on a watch," he says. "When I came to search the clothing of the poor fellow picked up, the timekeeper was found in his pocket. It was a gold one, and on the case was engraved an inscription, setting forth that it had been given to a sergeant in the Marines. Here was the clue sought after—the drowned man had evidently been in the army. The following morning I was on my way to Spring Gardens, when in

THE BRIDGE OF SIGHS.

K

not far to seek why it has been found necessary to establish a depôt here. We look up at the great bridge which spans the river at this point, named alas! with only too much truth, "The Bridge of Sighs." The dark water looks inviting to those burdened with trial and trouble, a place to receive those longing for rest and yearning for one word of sympathy. More suicides occur at this spot than at any other along the whole length of the river, though Whitehall Stairs and Adelphi Stairs are both notorious places, where such poor creatures end their existence. Some twenty-one suicides have been attempted at this point during the past year, and twenty-five bodies found.

As we step on the timber station the sensation is extremely curious to those used to the firm footing of the pavement. But Inspector Gibbons— a genial member of the river force — assures us that one soon becomes accustomed to the incessant rocking. Waterloo Police Station—familiar to all river pedestrians during the summer months, owing to the picturesque appearance it presents with its pots of geraniums and climbing fuchsias—is a highly interesting corner.

RESCUED!

passing down the Strand I saw a marine, whom I was half inclined to question. I did not, however, do so, but hurried on my sorrowful mission.

"On my arrival, I asked if they knew anything of Sergeant ——. Yes, they did. I must have passed him in the Strand, for he had gone to Coutts' Bank! I was perfectly bewildered. Here was the very man found drowned, still alive!

I could only wait until his return. Then the mystery was soon explained. It seemed that the sergeant had sold his gold watch in order to get a more substantial silver one, on condition that the purchaser should take the inscription off. This he failed to do, and he in his turn parted with the timekeeper to another buyer, who had finally committed suicide with the watch still in his pocket.

Our police galley is now alongside the station, just below Waterloo Bridge. It is

Just peep into the Inspector's room, and make friends with "Dick," the cat, upon whose shoulders rests the weight of four years and a round dozen pounds. Dick is a capital swimmer, and has been in the water scores of times. Moreover, he is a veritable feline policeman, and woe betide any trespassers of his own race and breed. When a cat ventures within the sacred precincts of the station, Dick makes friends with the intruder for the moment, and, in order to enjoy the breeze, quietly edges him to the extreme end of the platform, and suddenly pushes him overboard. "Another cat last night," is a common expression amongst the men here.

The Waterloo Police Station on occasion becomes a temporary hospital and a home together.

Only half an hour previous to our arrival there had been an attempted suicide, and in a little room, at the far end of the pier, there was every sign that efforts had only recently been successfully made to restore animation to a young fellow who had thrown himself off Blackfriars Bridge. He had been picked up by a passing skiff, and his head held above water until a steamboat passed by and took him on board.

Here is a bed in the corner, with comfortable-looking pillow and thick, warm blankets, where the unfortunate one is put to bed for a period, previous to being sent to the Infirmary, and afterwards charged. Close at hand is a little medicine chest, containing numerous medicine phials, a flask of stimulants, and a smelling-bottle. A dozen or so of tins, of all shapes and sizes, are handy. These are filled with hot water and placed in contact with the body of the person rescued from the river.

It is often an hour before anything approaching animation makes itself visible, and even four hours have elapsed before any sign has been apparent. The rescued one is laid upon a wooden board, below which is a bath, and rubbed by ready hands according to Dr. Sylvester's method, whose instructions are prominently displayed upon the wall, and are understood by all the police.

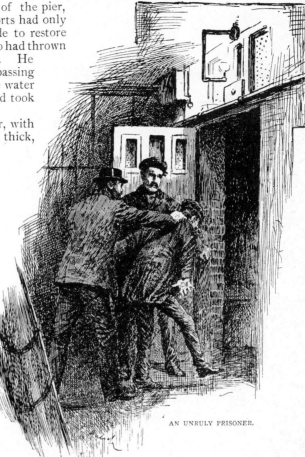

AN UNRULY PRISONER.

It will be noticed in the picture that two men are apparently about to undress the hapless creature who has attempted her own life. The first thought that will occur to the reader on looking at the illustration is, that a member of her own sex ought to to do this work. It must be remembered, however, that weeks may elapse without any such event, and there is no place at Waterloo Bridge where a woman could be kept constantly in waiting. Still, it is clearly not right that the men should do this duty, and we think they might be enabled to go to some house in the neighbourhood, in which arrangements had been made for the services of a woman in cases of emergency. We do not forget that great promptness is required at such times in order to resuscitate the body. But, when we remember that every branch in the police system on the Thames is so perfect, it seems a pity that some means cannot be devised.

Many remarkable things might be told about people who have been in this room. One poor fellow was once an inmate who was humorous to the last. When he was brought in, a pair of dumb-bells were found in his pocket, and a piece of paper on which was scrawled in charcoal the following :—

"Dear Bob,—I am going to drown myself. You will find me somewhere near Somerset House. I can't part with my old friends, Bob, so I'm going to take them with me. Good-bye."

The man was evidently an athlete, and the "old friends" referred to were the weighty dumb-bells.

Many have been picked up with their pockets full of granite stones or a piece of lead. One was found with the hands tied together with a silk handkerchief—a love-token which the forsaken one had used so pitifully. A woman, too, was discovered with a summons in her pocket, which was put down as the cause of her untimely end.

Remarkable are the escapes of would-be suicides. In one instance a woman threw herself off one of the bridges, and instead of falling into the water, jumped into a passing barge. She had a child in her arms. The little one died at Guy's Hospital, but the mother recovered. Some time ago a woman jumped off Westminster Bridge, and floated safely down to the Temple Stairs, where she was picked up. She had gone off the bridge feet first, the wind had caught her clothes, and by this means her head was kept up, and she was saved.

Perhaps, however, the strangest case and one of the most romantic, was that of Alice Blanche Oswald. Previous to committing suicide she wrote letters to herself, purporting to come from wealthy people in America, and setting forth a most heartrending history. Her death aroused a vast amount of public sympathy. A monument to her memory was suggested, and subscriptions were already coming in, when inquiries proved that her supposed friends in America did not exist, and that the story contained in the missives was a far from truthful one. She was nothing more than an adventuress.

As we glance in at the solitary cell, built on exactly the same principle as those at Wapping, in which eleven enterprising individuals have been accommodated at one time, we learn of the thousand and one odds and ends that are washed up—revolvers and rifles, housebreaking instruments which thoughtful burglars have got rid of ; the plant of a process for manufacturing counterfeit bank-notes, with some of the flimsy pieces of paper still intact. A plated cup was once picked up at Waterloo, which turned out to be the proceeds of a burglary at Eton College ; it is probable the cup floated all the way from the Thames at Windsor to Waterloo.

Forty-eight men are always on duty at this station, including four single men, whose quarters are both novel and decidedly cosy. This quartet of bachelors sleep in bunks, two above the others. The watch of one of the occupants is ticking away in one berth, whilst a clock is vieing with it next door. These men have each a separate locker for their clothes, boot-brushes, teapot, coffee-pot, food, &c. The men do all their own cleaning and cooking ; if you will, you may look into a kitchen in the corner, in which every pot and pan is as bright as a new pin.

But our time is up ; the chiming of " Big Ben " causes the genial inspector gently to remind us that we must be off, and once more we are seated in the boat, and, cutting right across the river, move slowly on our way to Greenwich, where the old *Royalist* is transformed into a station, a familiar institution some sixteen or seventeen years ago at Waterloo.

The whole scene is wonderfully impressive—not a sound is to be heard but the distant rumbling of the vehicles over London Bridge. Our men pause for a moment and rest their oars. The great wharves are deserted, the steamers and barges appear immovable as they lie alongside—there is no life anywhere or any sign of it. Again we get along, halting for a moment to look up at the old man-o'-war, the famous *Discovery*, which ventured out to the Arctic regions under Captain Nares. The old three-mast schooner—for the vessel is nothing more now, being used as a river carrier of the stores from the Victualling Yard at Deptford to the various dockyards —had on board when she went to colder regions a future member of the Thames Police : hence he was called " Arctic Jack " by his companions, a near relation to " Father Neptune," a cognomen bestowed upon another representative of the force, owing to the wealth of white beard which he possessed.

Past Deptford Cattle Market, the red lamps on the jetties light up the water ; a good pull and we are at Greenwich Steps, near to which is " The Ship," ever associated with the name of " whitebait." Our beat is ended, and a hearty " Good-night " is re-echoed by the men as we stand watching them on the river steps whilst they pull the first few strokes on their way home to Wapping.

Actors' Dressing Rooms.

THE robing apartments of actors are pleasant retreats. Quaint old prints, auto-graphed portraits and pictures, highly-prized pro-grammes, letters from cele-brities are as numerous as they are in-teresting, whilst every actor bids "good luck" cross his threshold by exhibiting his own particular horse-shoe in a conspicuous corner.

Where is a more picturesque room than that which Henry Irving enters nightly? Scarcely a dozen square inches of wall paper is to be seen—pictures are every-where. The eminent tragedian has a

was on his way to America. He turned up, however, at the Lyceum stage door four days afterwards, and it remains a mystery to this day as to whether Fussie came by road or rail.

Henry Irving's room is a comfortable apartment. The floor is covered with oil-cloth, and a huge rug imparts a cosy ap-pearance. Irving always uses the same chair to sit in when making up. It has broken down a score of times, but has been patched up again and again. In fact, the actor has almost a reverence for anything which is a connecting link with old associations.

Look at the costumes, for instance, hang-ing behind a door which leads to a very

MR. IRVING'S DRESSING-ROOM.

private entrance in Burleigh-street, and you may know when the actor is not far away, for "Fussie," a pet fox-terrier, always heralds his approach. "Fussie" has his own mat to sit on, and here he waits during the whole of the performance until after the second act, when he regularly looks up for his customary biscuit. It was "Fussie" who was lost at Southampton when Mr. Irving

unpretentious-looking wash-basin. There hangs the clothing of *The Master of Ravenswood*. The two Spanish hats with long feathers, the velvet coat and waistcoat with innumerable buttons, a quaint old crimson waistcoat, with elaborate silver work. Mr. Irving clings to an old coat so long as it will cling to him. He makes his clothes old—wears them during the day.

That old beaver hat was worn in "Charles I." and "The Dead Heart"—now it is the characteristic head-gear of *The Master of Ravenswood*. The hat worn in the last act did duty ten years ago in "The Corsican Brothers."

There, just by the long pier glass, is the old fashioned oak dressing-table, of a pattern associated with the days of King Arthur —in fact, the table has done duty in "Macbeth" in one of the banqueting scenes. Handle some of the veritable curiosities on it. The very looking-glass is tied up with string—it has reflected its owner's face for fourteen years, and went across the Atlantic with him. The old pincushion went as well. On a chair are the actor's eye-glasses, which he always uses when making up. Scissors, nail parers, &c., are about, whilst the paints lie in a little side cabinet by the looking-glass, and four diminutive gallipots are conspicuous, filled with the colours mostly used. A great tin box of crepe hair is also at hand, for Mr. Irving makes all his own moustaches. He gums a little hair on where needed and then works in colour to get the effect.

EUGENE ARAM'S LANTERN.

The wicker hand-basket is interesting. The dresser carries this to "the wings" when the actor needs a rapid change of "make-up." It has three compartments, holding a glass of water, powder puff, saucer containing fuller's earth, cold cream, hare's foot, lip salve, rouge, and a remarkably old comb and brush. Here is a striking collection of rings ; a great emerald —only a "stage" gem, alas !—is worn in "Louis XI." and "Richelieu," whilst here is one worn as *Doricourt* in the "Belle's Stratagem," the space where the stone ought to be being ingeniously filled up with blue sealing wax. These long pear-shaped pearl earrings are worn as *Charles I.*, such as all gay cavaliers were wont to wear.

You can handle the quaint old bull's-eye lantern which tradition says Eugene Aram carried on the night of the murder—for it is on the table. A piece of wick still remains and grease is visible—not as the morbid Aram left it, but as last used. The lantern itself is of stamped metal. The glass on either side is there, though that through which the light was seen in the centre has long since left. It is a highly interesting relic.

Be careful not to step into a big flower-pot saucer just close by, where "Fussie" drinks ; mind not to overturn what looks like a magnified pepper-box near the fire-place, but which, after all, only contains the dust which is "peppered" on to the actor's long boots, to make them look travel-stained and worn. Then walk round the room and admire the treasures.

There is a little gift sent from Denmark. In a neat oak frame is a picture of Elsinore, sprays of leaves from "Ophelia's brook," and a number of tiny stones and pebbles from "Hamlet's Grave." Here again is Kean, by Sir Thomas Lawrence, a small "Maclise," a sketch by Charles Matthews, Fechter— who used to dress in this very room himself—as *The Master of Ravenswood*, Ellen Terry as *Ophelia*, Sara Bernhardt, and John L. Toole. Variety is found in a pair of horseshoes, one of which Mr. Irving carried with him to America.

Over the crimson plush mantel-board is "Garrick in the Greenroom," and on either side a pair of ancient coloured prints of the one and only Joey Grimaldi, one of which represents him "as he appeared when he took his farewell benefit at Drury Lane Theatre on June 27, 1828," with pan and soap in his lap, arrayed in highly coloured garments, wonderfully made, and wearing a remarkably broad smile on his face. But to mention every one of Mr. Irving's treasures would be impossible.

The play over, he is in walking costume, cigar alight, and away in less than a quarter of an hour—"Fussie" with him, following faithfully in his steps.

Mr. Toole's room is exactly what everybody imagines it to be—cosy and homely, like its genial occupant. The casual passer-by over the iron grating in King William-street little thinks that he is throwing a momentary shadow over the very corner where Toole's washstand, soap and towel find a convenient lodging.

How simple everything is ! The little table in the centre where Toole sits down and religiously "drops a line," during the time he is not wanted in the piece, to all those unknown "young friends" who would tempt good fortune on the stage; the sofa covered with flowered cretonne; and in close proximity to the fireplace a

rising young actor who had only recently made his appearance—J. L. Toole by name.

Near a capital character sketch of Henry J. Byron, by Alfred Bryan, is an old playbill in a black ebony frame. This was the programme for one night:—

MR. TOOLE'S DRESSING-ROOM.

ricketty arm-chair in brown leather. The springs are broken, but what matter? That chair is Toole's, sir, and Royalty has occupied it many a time. Yes, nothing could be more simple than our own comedian's dressing-room. It is just a cosy parlour, and with Toole in the chair by the fire-side one would be loth to leave it.

The mantel-board has a clock in the centre, an ornament or two, and a bust of the occupant in his younger days. In a corner is the veritable umbrella used in *Paul Pry.* What a priceless collection of theatrical reminiscences meet the eye everywhere! There is a portrait group of a company of young actors who appeared in the original production of "Dearer than Life," at the New Queen's Theatre, Long-acre —Henry Irving, Charles Wyndham, John Clayton, Lionel Brough, John L. Toole, and Miss Henrietta Hodson, who afterwards became Mrs. Labouchere. A tolerably good cast! And here are portraits of a few actors taken years ago at Ryde, Isle of Wight, showing W. Creswick in a great Inverness cape, Benjamin Webster, S. Phelps, Paul Bedford, and a

THEATRE ROYAL, HAYMARKET.
MERCHANT OF VENICE.

The Drama in 3 Acts :
MIND YOUR OWN BUSINESS.

KEELEY WORRIED BY BUCKSTONE.
Mr. Keeley .... By himself.
Mr. Buckstone .... By himself.

To conclude with the laughable farce,
THE SPITALFIELDS WEAVER.
Simmons .... Mr. John L. Toole.
(*His first appearance on any stage*).

Many a white satin programme is about, and the tenant of the little dressing-room of King William-street is represented in many parts. Just by the door is Mr. Liston as *Paul Pry*, arrayed in bottle-green coat, big beaver hat, and armed with the inevitable umbrella—"just called to ask you how your tooth was."

An excellent portrait represents John Billington as *John Peerybingle* in "Dot," underneath which are penned some noteworthy lines : "I don't want anybody to tell me my fortune. I've got one of the best little wives alive, a happy home over my head, a blessed baby, and a cricket on my hearth."

Certainly what Mr. W. S. Gilbert would term "a highly respectable" entrance is that which leads to Mr. Beerbohm Tree's dressing-room. The stage door is in Suffolk-street, and until Mr. Tree's tenancy of the Haymarket Theatre, there was an old clause in the lease setting forth that whenever Royalty visited the theatre they should have the right to enter by that way. Buckstone lived here—his dressing-room still remains. It is a quaint corner near the stage, now used by the actors as a smoking-room. The walls are covered with red paper, relieved by one or two decidedly ancient paintings. Buckstone's iron safe—wherein the renowned comedian was wont to store his money — is still visible ; but the money-bags are there no longer ; their place being occupied by sundry jars of tobacco and a church-warden or two. Only on one occasion has Mr. Tree found it necessary to use this room. The corpulency of the bibulous *Falstaff* prevented the actor from conveniently coming down the stairs which lead from his own room to the stage—hence *Falstaff* was attired in this apartment.

The sound of the overture is just beginning as we hurriedly follow Mr. Tree in the direction of his room. Though he has been singled out as a very master of the art of transferring the face into the presentment of character, it is a fact that Mr. Tree never sits down to dress until the overture has started, and attaches less importance to his make-up than to any other portion of the actor's art.

He throws himself into a chair of a decided " office " pattern, in front of a triple

glass which reflects all positions of his face. The sticks of paint are arranged on a small Japanese tray, and the various powders in tin boxes. Everything about the room is quiet and unassuming—a washstand near the window, a few odd wooden-back chairs. The room is regarded rather as a workshop than a lounging-room, and it certainly possesses that appearance, though not without a certain pleasant cosiness.

The actor's fingers have evidently been recently at work on the lengthy pier-glass. Young Mr. Irving has just been in. He wanted some idea of a make-up for *King John.* Mr. Tree gave him one by taking a

MR. BEERBOHM TREE'S DRESSING-ROOM.

stick of grease paint and sketching it in outline on the glass. A number of still unanswered letters are lying about—some of them delightfully humorous missives from "stage-struck" young people. One is positively from a footman. It runs :—

" DEAR SIR,—I want to be an actor, so thought I would write to you. I am tall and dark, and have been a footman for five years in a nobleman's family. I have just had a hundred pounds left me, and if you will give me a part in one of your pieces I will give you fifty pounds of it. Write by return, as I have already given notice.—Your obedient servant,   ——

" P.S.—Mark the letter private."

MR. HARE'S DRESSING-ROOM.

In a corner lies the peak cap worn as *Demetrius* in "The Red Lamp"; here the cloth cap, gaily decorated with poppies, corn and feathers, used in "The Ballad Monger." Over the door is a gigantic horseshoe, measuring at least a couple of feet from top to bottom. This was placed here by Mrs. Bancroft.

Just at this moment a magnificent bull-dog—whose appearance we had not previously noticed—turns lazily on a mat under the dressing-table. This is "Ned," rechristened "Bully Boy." The dog plays a prominent part in the piece now running at the Haymarket.

A tap at the door. A voice cries, "Mr. Tree"—and hurriedly applying a line here and there about the eyes, as we accompany the actor to the stage, he has something interesting to say regarding "making-up." He rather laughs at the idea, and is perplexed to understand the reason why his facial paintings are so commented upon. He is always the last to reach the theatre. "The less make-up, the better," he observes. "The art of acting is not a matter of painting the face, for a very plain person can in a few seconds become extremely good-looking and *vice versâ ;* it is what comes from within—what the player feels. It is his imagination which really illuminates the

face, and not what he has put on it with hare's foot and pencil."

A peculiar interest is attached to the visit which we made to Mr. John Hare's room at the Garrick Theatre. Mr. Hare has been on the stage for twenty-six years, and previous to our finding him seated in his great arm-chair by the fireplace, had never been interviewed. Hence the few words he said, as he played with a cigarette, become particularly notable.

"I have been acting now for twenty-six years. I was for ten years with Mrs. Bancroft at the Prince of Wales's, and have been some twelve or thirteen years in management."

"What is your favourite part, Mr. Hare ? "

"The present one in 'A Pair of Spectacles,'" is the reply. "I take about a month to study up a character. I always wear the clothes I am going to play in for some time previously, so as to get them to my figure. The longest time I ever bestowed on a make-up was in 'The Profligate.' I took half an hour over it."

Mr. Hare has really two rooms. The

big one is used for an office as much as possible, where the actor does all his correspondence. Note the old-fashioned high wire fender, the heavy plush curtains, and elaborate rosewood furniture. It is a most artistic apartment. Those speaking-tubes communicate with the stage door, prompter, box office, and acting manager.

The pictures which adorn the walls are as varied as they are valuable. Here may be

MR. HARE'S INNER ROOM.

found Leslie Ward's caricature of Corney Grain and of George Grossmith, together with an old engraving of Garrick, after R. E. Pine, published in 1818. Just by the glass is one of the few photos of Compton, in frock coat and plaid tie. Many a reminiscence of the Hare and Kendal management is about, and on the mantel-board of ebony and gold—over which rests the customary horse-shoe with the initials J. H. in the centre—portraits in silver frames of members of Mr. Hare's family are to be seen.

But by far the most attractive corner is a little room, scarcely large enough for two people to stand in, which branches off from the more spacious apartment. There, hanging up, is the light suit worn as *Benjamin Goldfinch*, with the long black coat which flaps about so marvellously—the actor finds plenty of "character" even in a coat —and the shepherd's-plaid trousers.

The looking-glass is of walnut, with electric lights on either side shaded with metal leaves. In front of this he sits, amidst a hundred little oddments. Here are tiny bottles of medicine and quinine—for the actor being is a firm believer in the properties of this traditional strength-reviver. The little room is as comfortable as it well can be, and has a thoroughly domesticated air about it.

There are many things to notice as we pass through the passages on our way toward Mr. Charles Wyndham's room at the Criterion; programmes and play-bills in German and Russian of "David Garrick" —in fact the passages are literally decorated with mementoes of the clever comedian's admirable impersonation of this character. A bronze of the actor as *Davy* raising the glass on high, and a massive silver loving cup, engraved "Garrick," is mounted on a pedestal bearing the inscription "Charles Wyndham, Von Direktor Lautenberg, Residencz Theatre, Berlin, December, 1887." Prints and pictures typical of Russian life are freely displayed. And here is an exceptional curiosity, and one which is doubtless highly treasured. In a modest oak frame is a piece of paper which once served to settle a little dispute, which is historical among things theatrical :—

"Mr. Bedford wages two gallons of claret with Mr. Williams, that Mr. Garrick did not play upon ye stage in ye year 1732 or before."

Then follows the suggestive word "Paid," and below it are the words :—

"I acted upon Goodman's Fields Theatre for ye first time in ye year 1741.
                                    "D. GARRICK.
"Witness,
    "SOMERSET DRAPER."

Mr. Wyndham's room has one thing about it which distinguishes it from all similar apartments in London. It is next to the stage, and by pulling up a little red blind he can see through an aperture just what is going on, and know exactly when his services are required.

The room is square, divided by a curtain. Strange to say, not a single portrait of a brother actor is apparent ; but, whilst the actor paints his face, he can see many an invitation to dinner negligently thrust in the edges of the gilt frame. The dressing-table which occupies nearly the whole length of one end of the room is fully supplied with countless colours, whilst a little tray is positively brimming over with all patterns of collar studs. An egg is handy ; it is intended for the hair, as Mr. Wyndham and wigs have never agreed, There is a writing-table and a chair or two, and an elaborate inlaid rosewood escritoire is in a corner, against which Mr. Wyndham stands for his portrait in the character of *Dazzle*, with his flowered waistcoat, frilled front, and hanging fob.

Nor must the apartment in which Mr. Wyndham entertains his friends be passed unnoticed. This is a room overlooking Piccadilly, and capable of seating some twenty or twenty-five persons. It was dark when we entered, but the next instant the electric light was switched on, and an apartment was presented which may be singled out as the only one of its kind ever built.

We were standing in the middle of a first-class cabin of a ship. Not a solitary item was wanting to complete the illusion. The ceiling was built low, and every article of furniture was made on sea-going principles, even down to the table. The walls are of walnut, the panels between being lined with exquisite sateen. Though one or two windows look out on to Piccadilly Circus, there are many port-holes about, all draped with old gold plush curtains. The upholstery consists principally of a series of settees of light blue plush, which go round the sides of the room.

The looking-glass over the mantelpiece is typical of a cabin. It is surrounded, in the form of a framework, by a cable, the ends of which are fastened off by diminutive anchors. Exactly in the centre, in an elaborate frame, is the programme used on the occasion of the performance of " David Garrick," which Mr. Wyndham and his brother actors gave before the Prince and Princess of Wales at Sandringham some years ago.

The very lamps suspended from the ceiling are made to sway to and fro in case of rough and windy weather. The whole thing is an ingenious idea, delightfully carried out, and to-night Mr. Wyndham's cabin is seen at its best. There is to be a supper-party at the conclusion of the performance downstairs, and the tables for the time being are burdened down with every luxury. Fairy lamps are peeping out amongst the pines and hot-house grapes, and the lamps hanging from the roof are surrounded with flowers and ferns, whilst the electric light shines out brilliantly from amongst the blossoms.

MR. WYNDHAM'S DRESSING-ROOM.

A Day with an East-End Photographer.

HERE y'are now, on'y sixpence for yer likeness, the 'ole thing, 'strue's life. Come inside now, won'tcher? No waitin'. Noo instanteraneous process."

Thus, with the sweet seductiveness of an East-end tout, was a photographer endeavouring to inveigle 'Arry and 'Arriet into his studio, which was situated—well, "down East som'ere," as the inhabitants themselves would describe the locality. It was somewhere near the Docks; somewhere, you may be sure, close bordering upon that broad highway that runs 'twixt Aldgate and the Dockgates, for within those boundaries the tide of human life flows most strongly, and the photographer hoped, by stationing himself there, to catch a few of the passersby, thrown in his way like flotsam and jetsam. He was not disappointed in this expectation. While daylight lasted there was generally a customer waiting in his little back parlour, enticed thither by the blandishments of the tout outside.

The establishment was not prepossessing to an eye cultivated in the appearance of the artistic façades of photographers in the West. The frontage consisted of a little shop, with diminutive windows, which it

THE ESTABLISHMENT.

was the evident desire of the proprietor to make the most of by engaging in other commercial pursuits.

There seemed to be an incongruity in the art of the photographer being associated with the sale of coals, firewood, potatoes, sweets, and gingerbeer, but the East-enders apparently did not trouble themselves to consider this in the least. There was, indeed, a homely flavour about this miscellaneous assortment of useful and edible articles, which commended itself to their mind. What was more natural than that 'Arry, having indulged in the luxury of a photograph, should pursue his day's dissipation by treating his 'Arriet to a bottle of the exhilarating " pop," to say nothing of a bag of sweets to eat on their holiday journey.

The coals, firewood, and potato department, so far from being regarded as in any way derogatory to the photographer's profession, was rather calculated to impress the natives, who were accustomed to look upon a heap of coals —to say nothing of the firewood and potatoes—as a material sign of prosperity.

So far as the photographer was concerned it was a matter of necessity as well as choice that he came to be thus associated, for it transpired that he had married the buxom woman, whom we now see behind the counter, at a time when he was trying hard to make ends meet in the winter season, when photography is at a discount. She, on the other hand, had a thriving little business of the general nature we have indicated, and was mourning the loss of the partner who had inaugurated the shop, and for a time had shared with her his joys and sorrows. The photographer had won her heart by practising his art on Hampstead Heath the last Bank Holiday, and the happy acquaintance thus formed had ripened into one of such mutual affection that the union was consummated, and another department was added to the little general business by the conversion of the yard at the back into a photographic studio.

The placards announcing the price of coals and firewood, and the current market rates of potatoes, were elevated to the topmost panes of the window, and the lower half was filled with a gorgeous array of specimen portraits in all the glory of their tinsel frames.

IN THE SHOW CASE.

From that day the shop was a huge attraction, and the proprietor of the wax-work show over the way cast glances of ill-concealed envy and jealousy at the crowd which had deserted his frontage for the later inducements opposite.

The incoming vessels from foreign ports brought many visitors, and generally a few customers. To the foreign element the window was especially fascinating. Many a face of strange mien stared in at the window, and the photographer being somewhat of an adept with an instantaneous camera, would often secure a "snap shot" of some curious countenance, the owner of which could not be enticed within. These would duly appear in the show cases, and served as decoys to others of the same nationality.

There was the solemn-faced Turk in showy fez, and with dainty cigarette 'twixt his fingers, who surveyed the window with immutable countenance, and was imper-vious to all the unction of the tout. This latter worthy was not aware that it was against the religion of the "unspeakable Turk" to be photographed, or he would not have wasted his energy on such an unpromising customer.

The negro sailor was apparently struck with the presentments of the other members of his race, but asseverated that he was "stone broke," and did not own a cent to pay for a photograph. He had spent such small earnings as he had received, and was now on his way back to his vessel. "Me no good, me no money," he told the tout, who turned away from him in disgust.

There has so far been a good many passers-by to-day for every likely customer, and the tout is almost in despair. "Rotters," he mutters; "not a blessed tanner among 'em."

Ah! here's his man, though, and he is on the alert for his prey, as he sees a dapper little figure with unmistakable Japanese features come sauntering down the street. He is dressed in the most approved style of the East-end tailor, who no doubt has assured him that he is a "reg'lar masher." So evidently thinks the little Jap, as he shoots his cuffs forward, flourishes his walking cane, and displays a set of ivory white teeth in his guileless Celestial smile. The tout rubs his hands with a business-like air of satisfaction as he sees the victim safely handed over to the tender mercies of the operator within. "Safe for five bobs' worth, that 'un," he soliloquises, winking at no one in particular, but possibly just to relieve his feelings by the force of habit.

The next customer attracted was an Ayah, or Hindoo nurse, a type often to be seen in the show-case of the East-end photographer. These women find their way to England through engagements as nurses to Anglo-Indian families coming home, and they work their way back by re-engagements to families outward bound. Whenever a P. & O. boat arrives there will most probably be seen one or more of these women, whose stately walk and Oriental attire at once attract attention.

Prominent also among the natives who find their way up from the Docks are the Malay sailors, in their picturesque white dresses. Sometimes the photographer secures a couple for a photo, but as a rule they have little money. "Like all the rest o' them blessed haythens," says the tout, "not a bloomin' meg among a 'ole baker's dozen of 'em."

The faces of such types are not, however, interesting to the East-enders. Their interest in the window display is only heightened when familiar faces make their appearance in the tinsel frames. There was, for instance, positive excitement in the neighbourhood when a highly-coloured portrait of the landlord of a well-known beershop in the same street was added to the collection.

Everyone recognised the faithfulness at once, though it was irreverently hinted that in the colouring the exact shade of the gentleman's nose had not been faithfully copied.

One can imagine the feelings of pride with which the photographer had posed his worthy neighbour, who had arrayed himself in all the glory of his Sunday best suit.

"Head turned a little this way, please! Yes—now — look at this—yes — now, look pleasant!"

Everything would have gone well at this point, but the dog, which it was intended should form an important adjunct to the picture, and symbolically typify the sign of the house—"The Jolly Dog"—set up a mournful howl, and made desperate efforts to get away from the range of that uncanny instrument in front of him. However, the photographer waited for a more favourable moment, and while the dog was considering the force of his master's remarks, the exposure was successfully made. The result was regarded as quite a *chef d'œuvre* in the eyes of those who stopped to gaze at it as it hung in a place of honour in the window of the little front shop.

"NOW, LOOK PLEASANT!"

The "reg'lar" East-enders, as distinguished from the foreign element, were, indeed, very easy to please; but, unfortunately, they were not the mainstay of the photographer's business. He must needs look for other customers to eke out a living. And here his difficulties began. He had to be careful not to take a certain low type of Jewish features in profile, for the foreign Jew, once he has been acclimatised, does not like to look "sheeny"; and the descendants of Ham—euphemistically classed under the generic term of "gentlemen of colour"—were always fearful lest their features should come out too dark. One young negro who came to be photographed expressly stipulated that he should not be made to look black. To obviate this difficulty, the photographer wets his customer's face with water, so as to present a shiny appearance to the lens of the camera, and a brighter result is thus secured. On this particular occasion the ingenious dodge failed, and the vain young negro loudly denounced it as representing him a great deal blacker than he was in the flesh. Indeed, the tears sparkled in his eyes as he protested that he was "no black nigger." There is a subtle distinction, mark you, between a "nigger" and a "black nigger" in the mind of a "coloured person," and no

Yrouur

Too, too black.

A. Pole

greater insult can be levelled at him than to apply the latter epithet.

The tout's thoughts are soon distracted by the appearance of a German fraulein, evidently of very recent arrival in England, who is admiring the photos in the window. She is arrayed in a highly-coloured striped dress, which is not of a length that would be accepted at the West-end, for it reaches only to the ankles, and shows her feet encased in a clumsy pair of boots. An abnormally large green umbrella which she carries is another characteristic feature that seems inseparable from women of this type.

The tout has a special method of alluring the women folk within the studio. He has a piece of mirror let into one of the tinsel frames which he carries in his hand as specimens. He holds this up before the woman's face, and asks her to observe what a picture she would make. This little artifice seldom fails to attract the women, whatever their nationality, for vanity is vanity all the world over.

John Chinaman is quite as easily satisfied, and the tout has no difficulty in drawing him within, but the drawback to his custom is that he seldom has any money, or, if he has any, is not inclined to part with it. It is just a "toss-up," as the tout says, whether he will pay, if he gets the Celestial inside, though it is worth the risk when business is not very brisk.

Here is one fine specimen of a Celestial coming along. Western civilisation, as yet, has made no impression upon him, and he looks for all the world the Chinaman of the willow-pattern plate in the window of the tea shop. John falls an easy prey to the tout, who ushers him inside, and whispers to the "Guv'nor" in a mysterious aside: "Yew du 'im for nothin', if ye can't get him to brass up. Lots o' Chaneymen about to-day, an' 'e'll advertise the business." The customer is thereupon posed with especial favour, the photographer feeling that the reputation of the business in the Celestial mind depends on the success of this effort. Chinese accessories are called into play; John Chinaman is seated in a bamboo chair, against a bamboo table, supporting a flower vase which looks suspiciously as though it had once served as a receptacle for preserved ginger. Overhead is hung a paper lantern, and the background is turned round so that the stretcher frame of the canvas may give the appearance of a

Celestial Delight

Jintyped Types

Chinese interior. There is no need to tell the sitter to look pleasant, for his features at once expand into that peculiar smile which Bret Harte has described as " child-like and bland."

The photo is duly completed and handed over to the customer for his inspection and approval. He manifests quite a childish delight, and is about to depart with it, when he is reminded by word and sign that he has not paid. John very well understands the meaning of it all, but smiles vacuously. When, however, the photographer begins to look threatening, he whines in his best English that he has no money. The photographer slaps him all round in the hope of hearing a jingle of concealed coins, but to no purpose. " Another blessed specimen, gratis ! " he mutters, as he allows his unprofitable customer to depart with the photo, in the hope that it will attract some of his fellow-countrymen to the studio. This seems quite likely, for the Chinaman goes off in a transport of delight. He stops now and again to survey the photo, and the appearance of it evidently gives such satisfaction that he goes dancing off like a child to show it to his Celestial brethren. They

straightway resolve also to go and have a photograph for nothing.

A group of chattering Chinamen soon appear in front of the photographer's shop, with the late customer in the midst explaining how the trick is done. It seems to be finally resolved that they should go in one at a time, the others waiting outside. One young member of the party accordingly steps forward, and the tout, delighted to find the bait has so soon taken, never considers the possibility that this customer likewise has no money.

The same scene is enacted as in the previous case, but when it comes to the point of paying for the photo, and John Chinaman is found to be absolutely penniless, there is an unrehearsed ending to the little comedy. The proprietor of the photographic establishment seizes the Chinaman by the collar and drags him into the front shop, where the tout, in instant comprehension of the state of affairs, takes the offender in hand and very neatly kicks him over the doorstep, whence he falls into the midst of his compatriots, who all take to their heels, screaming in a high-pitched key. The tout looks at their rapidly retreating figures with a countenance eloquently expressive of mingled sorrow and anger, vowing vengeance on any other of " them haythen

Chaynees " who might choose to try the game of securing photos for nothing. " Ought to be all jolly well drowned in the river," he remarks to his colleague indoors.

On the other hand, the heavy-browed, gaunt-cheeked, male Teuton is not

" KICKED OUT."

scarf ; his boots are big and heavy, and his trousers several inches too short for him.

In a short time, however, he will blossom forth into a billycock hat, with broad and curly brim of the most approved East-end cut ; patent leather boots to match, and a very loud red tie. The hungry look has by this time given way to a sleek, well-fed nature,

A TEUTON.

so easy to attract, but the photographer can trust the course of things to bring him eventually to the studio. When first imported he stares in at the window in a stolid, indifferent manner. His face has a hungry look, and is shadowed by a heavily slouched hat; his hair is unkempt; he wears an untidy and unclean

and he will stroll along with a Teuton sweet-heart, likewise transformed very much from her former self. The short, gaudily-striped dress has given way to the latest "'krect thing" in East-

SOME FOREIGN IMMIGRANTS

AN ORIENTAL.

end fashion, and the green stuff umbrella has gone the way of the striped skirt, to be replaced by the latest novelty in " husband beaters." Then it is that the Teutonic 'Arry and Arriet patronise the photographer, and rejoice his heart with, perhaps, a five-shilling order.

The show-case of the East-end photographer gives one a very fair idea of the evolution of the foreign immigrant.

The tout seemed to know the history of every person whose photograph was displayed in the show-case, and he was rattling it off to us at a rate which precluded any possibility of storing it up in our memory, when a slight diversion was created by a coster's barrow, drawn by a smart little pony, being driven up to the front of the photographer's. The driver was Mr. Higgins, we learnt, and the other occupants of the barrow were Mrs. Higgins and the infant son and heir to the Higgins' estate, which was reputed to be something considerable in the costermongers' way, as was evidenced by the fact that Mr. Higgins was enabled to keep a pony to draw his barrow. Mrs. Higgins had determined that 'Enery—*ætat* one year and eight months—should have his photograph taken and afterwards be glorified in a coloured enlargement. Mr. Higgins had assented to this being done regardless of expense. It was a weighty responsibility for the photographer, who always considered the taking of babies was not his strong point. But he reflected upon the increased fame which would accrue to his business if he was successful, and he determined to do it or perish in the attempt.

"YOUNG HIGGINS."

He made hasty preparations by selecting the most tempting stick of toffy he could find in the sweetstuff window, and the tout was instructed to procure from a neighbouring toy shop a doll, a rattle, a penny trumpet, and other articles dear to the juvenile mind.

The youthful Higgins was duly placed in a chair, behind which Mrs. Higgins was ensconced with a view to assisting the photographer by preserving a proper equilibrium in the sitter, and also ensuring confidence in the infantile mind.

So far, the child had been quietly sucking his thumb and surveying the studio with an interested air, but no sooner was his attention directed to the photographer than a distrustful frown settled upon his face, and his irritation at the photographer's presence found expression in a yell of infantile wrath. The more the photographer tried to conciliate by flourishing the toys the more the child yelled. The photographer danced and sung, and blew the penny trumpet, and was about to give up the operation in despair, when it dawned on him that he had forgotten the toffy stick. It was produced, and had its effect. On being assured by Mrs. Higgins, behind the chair, that the "ducksy darling would have its toffy stick," the youthful sitter held that prospective joy with his tear-glistening eye, and the photographer seizing a favourable moment performed the operation with a sigh of satisfaction. Baby Higgins had its toffy stick, Mrs. Higgins had a pleasing photo of her infant offspring, and the photographer proudly congratulated himself on having so successfully performed his task. The production of such elaborate efforts as the coloured enlargements was, however, attended with disadvantages and disappointments at times. It was hard to give entire satisfaction to such exacting critics in these matters as the East-end folk, and there was always the risk that the picture might be thrown upon his hands if not liked.

Taking it all round, his time was much more profitably employed out of doors on high days and holidays, in taking sixpenny "tintypes" "while you wait."

We have seen him on a Bank Holiday beaming with good luck. He has started out early in the morning with the intention of proceeding to Hampstead, but instead of going direct thither, he pitches his camera near the walls of the Docks, and manages to catch a good many passers-by before they have had the opportunity of spending their money in the pleasures of a London Bank Holiday. Here he has succeeded in inducing 'Arry and 'Arriet to have their photos taken.

Such is a chapter in the life of an East-end photographer. To-day he may be doing a "roaring" business, but to-morrow he may be reduced to accepting the twopences and threepences of children who club together and wait upon him with a demand that he will take "Me, an' Mary Ann, an' little Mickey all for thruppence." He invariably assents, knowing that, though there can be little profit, the photo will create a feeling of envy in the minds of other children who will decide on having a "real tip topper" at sixpence.

The stock-in-trade of an East-end photographer is not a very elaborate one. He may pick up the whole apparatus second-hand for about £5, and the studio and fittings are not expensive. The thin metal plates cost not more than 10s. per gross, and the tinsel binding frames about 3s. per gross, while the chemicals amount to an infinitesimal sum on each plate. On a good day a turnover of £2 to £3 may be made, but there are many ups and downs, and trials of temper and patience, to say nothing of the unhealthy nature of the business, all going to make up many disadvantages associated with the life of an East-end photographer.

Old Stone Signs of London.

THOUGH the predictions of John Dryden were not always fortunate, one stanza in the "Annus Mirabilis," 1666, which refers to the future of London City, may here be appropriately quoted :—

> " More great than human now and more August,
> New deified she from her fires does rise :
> Her widening streets on new foundations trust,
> And, opening, into larger parts she flies."

It may be observed that Augusta was the Roman name for London.

Now of the old stone signs of London yet extant, one or two only bear date anterior to the Great Fire. Many of those which still remain, fixed either on the outside walls or within the houses they originally marked, are undated, but their age may be guessed with a tolerable degree of accuracy. It is also known that the custom of denoting houses by carved stone signs built into the outer walls did not come into general use until the rebuilding of the city subsequent to the year 1666.

The inconvenience of the old swinging signs, which blocked the daylight, and which, by their creaking noises, made day and night alike hideous, had long been felt—nay, more, their danger to passersby, when wind and decay had caused a downfall, had been not a few times painfully apparent. Hence the Act of Charles II., which forbade swinging signboards, was both wise and salutary. The signboards, however, died hard, and prints as late as the middle of the eighteenth century show the streets full of them. But signs had their use in those days of unnumbered streets, and it was not until the numbering of the houses was enforced that the quaint, historic,

BOY AND PANYER.

and, in some cases, even highly artistic, landmarks vanished.

As years have rolled by, the stone signs themselves, built though they were into the walls of the houses, have in a great measure disappeared. Some are luckily preserved in the Guildhall Library Museum, others are in private hands, many have been carted away as rubbish during rebuilding, and only a few now remain *in situ*. It is with these few that this paper is now concerned, and of which illustrations are given.

The use of the curious sign known as the "Boy and Pannier," in Panyer-alley, is threefold. It was a street sign, a trade sign, and also, it would seem, a landmark. Stow, writing in 1598, mentions a street sign there, probably the upper portion only of the present sign. He writes, " . . . Is another passage out of Pater Noster row, and is called, of such a sign, Panyar Alley, which cometh out into the north over against St. Martins Lane." Along this alley the bakers' boys were wont to sit, with their baskets or panniers of bread exposed for sale, the sale of loaves at the bakers' shops for some reasons being prohibited by law. On the lower slab there yet remains a barely legible inscription, which in modern English runs thus :—

> When you have sought the city round,
> Yet still this is the highest ground.
> August 26, 1688.

Cheapside and its tributaries are, as times go, rather rich in stone signs. On the external wall of No. 37 may be seen a well carved swan with collar and chain. This is a sign of heraldic origin without doubt; it was, in fact, one of the badges of Henry IV., and was also heraldically one of the charges of Buckingham, Gloster, and others. Hitherto, however, efforts to trace the exact history of this sign have been without avail. Far different is it with the White Bear, now to be seen within the house of business of Messrs. Gow, No. 47, Cheapside. This most interesting sign was discovered while making alterations as lately as 1882. The house itself stands at the corner of Soper's-lane (modern designation, Queen-street), and was once the shop of the far-famed

THE SWAN.

merchant, Sir Baptist Hicks, Kt., subsequently Viscount Campden. Baptist Hicks was the successful son of a wealthy father, and succeeded to what was in those days a most thriving silk mercer's business. His career is remarkable in more ways than one, for though a favourite at Court, immensely wealthy and knighted, he was the first London merchant who after knighthood took the resolution to still continue in business.

WHITE BEAR.

It is also worthy of notice that the stone figure of the bear faces in the opposite direction to all other heraldic signs now standing in London. At No. 28, Budge-row, will be found one of the best preserved of all the London signs, "The Leopard" (otherwise Lizard or Lazarde). This is the crest of the Worshipful Company of Skinners, and as Budge-row took its name

from the skin of newly-born lamb, which was termed Budge, the origin of this sign can be in no way a matter of doubt. The Skinners' Hall, too, was close by, and quite early in the fourteenth century it may be noted that enactments were in force against the wearing of "cloth furred with Budge or Wool" by persons (women) of inferior rank.

Lower Thames-street, known in the time of Stow as Stock Fishmonger-street, still possesses two very good examples of signs : one, the "Bear," with its collar and chain, carved in very high relief, and surmounted by initials and date (1670).

On the borders of Islington and Clerkenwell there are a group of signs which belong to houses celebrated in past days. The first is the "Old Red Lion." Here there are two carved shields, one of which

THE LEOPARD.

only is antique—*i.e.*, that on the north gable. This house has memories and traditions both literary and artistic. Within its walls Tom Paine wrote the "Rights of Man." This is, however, a questionable honour. Here Hogarth was wont to stay, and has even introduced its gables into one of his prints—"Evening." The house, too, was the haunt at times of Thomson, Goldsmith, and Johnson.

Another sign is the "Pelican," of which there is an example in Aldermanbury. The fabulous story of the pelican "vulning" (*i.e.*, wounding) its breast to feed its young endured for ages, and even as late as the reign of George I., at Peckham Fair, there was advertised to be on view "A pelican that suckles her young with her heart's blood, from Egypt." In the same district as the "Pelican," at the corner of Addle-street, E.C., may be seen yet another "Bear"—how popular as sign:

BEAR AND CHAIN.

THE BEAR.

Company, to whom the house was left in 1568 by John Craythorne. The "Belle Sauvage Inn," over the origin of whose name and sign so much antiquarian ink has been spilt, vanished years ago. This hostelry was memorable among other things

and how enduring these bears seem! This carving is dated 1670 (not 1610), and bears initials N.T.E. The N., which is the surname, is reversed; the T. and the E. standing in all probability, as was customary, for the Christian names of the builder and his wife. The "Elephant and Castle," irreverently called the "Pig and Pepper-box," in Belle Sauvage-yard, is the crest of the Cutlers'

THE PELICAN.

for being opposite the spot at which the rebel Wyat rested on the occasion of his unsuccessful attempt to penetrate Ludgate. It was also a celebrated stopping-place for the northern carriers. In Belle Sauvage-yard for a time dwelt Grinling Gibbons, and there he carved, according to Walpole, "a plot of flowers which shook surprisingly with the motion of the coaches that passed by."

Two or three outlying stone signs remain now to be mentioned. One is the

THE OLD RED LION.

THE ELEPHANT AND CASTLE.

"Cock and Serpents," at No. 16, Church-lane, Chelsea. This sign, evidently religious in its origin, is very remarkable, both in its design and also from its date, 1652. It does not appear to have any history, though the road in which it is to be found teems with memories of not a few of England's worthies. Another, the sign of the "Dog and Duck," now built into the garden wall of Bethlem

DOG AND DUCK.

COCK AND SERPENTS.

the corner of Leather-lane, Hatton Garden. There appear to be doubts whether the present sign is the original, but as one branch of sign lore deals with signs appro-

priate to places, it may be well to mention this one, which is certainly of respectable antiquity, as an example. Space is wanting for more than mere mention of the "Marygold" of Messrs. Child's, the "Golden Bottle" of Messrs. Hoare's, and the three quaint iron squirrels of Messrs. Gosling's. Nor can the traditions of the ancient "Cock" Tavern in Fleet-street, with its carved wooden sign (possibly the work of Gibbons), be here related. The writer, however, may perhaps be permitted in conclusion to acknowledge with grati-tude his indebtedness to the only standard book on the subject, and also to kind assist-ance rendered to him by many with whom he has come in contact while tramping the now modern streets of our historic metro-polis in search of its ancient signs.

Hospital in Southwark, is important from the fact that it records the precise sport (duck hunting) which was the attraction of the house, and also because on the same stone, and dated 1716, we find the arms of the Borough and Southwark—a conjunc-tion of which the history of signboards offers no other example.

One illustration is given of a sign which is not stone, *i.e.*, the "Leather Bottle," at

THE LEATHER BOTTLE.

Child Workers in London.

THIS article does not profess to be an exhaustive account of all the employments in which London children are engaged. The limits of a magazine article do not allow of a full and detailed account of this very comprehensive subject. No individual or body of individuals has any precise information about the hundreds of children engaged as ballet dancers, acrobats, models, and street venders, to give only a few names in the vast army of child workers.

Nothing can be harder and drearier than the lot of little servants, employed in many cases in lodging - houses. They are on their feet all day long, at everyone's beck and call, and never expected to be tired or to sit down properly for a meal; the food is of the poorest quality; they have heavy weights to drag up and down stairs in the shape of coal - scuttles, and the inevitable strapping baby; their sleeping apartment is as often as not a disgraceful hole, and such requisites to health as are generally considered necessary in the shape of exercise, fresh air, and baths are unknown quantities. There is a strong prejudice against the "factory girl" in many quarters, and "service" is indiscriminately extolled as far more suitable for a respectable girl of the lower classes. It would be, if there were any chance of the docker's child or the coster's child obtaining a decent

A CHILD NURSE.

situation; but, as a matter of fact, the life of the much-pitied match-worker is infinitely easier than that of these little drudges. At eight o'clock the factory girl is at any rate free to get out into the open air for a couple of hours, or to sit down and rest. The little "general" is never free. One child told me—she was the daughter of a docker who was the happy owner of eleven children, and was herself an under-fed, anæmic-looking creature—that she got up at six every morning to "make the gen'l'm's brakfast—it was a lodging-house; after that there's the steps, 'ouse work, peeling potatoes, and sich like, till dinner. I never sits down till we 'ave a cup o' tea after the lodgers 'ave 'ad their suppers. But the missis—oh, she is a nice, kind laidy, and she works with me, she do."

"I suppose," I said, "you are able to get out on Sundays?"

"Once a month I goes 'ome, but I nusses the baby on Sunday, as we ain't so busy. 'E's such a beauty; I'll ask missis if I can bring 'im down; e' can't walk by 'isself." And off darted the little maid to the top of the house as if she were not on her thin legs from morn to night, returning presently with a huge and well-fed baby, about three times as fat as herself. I am bound to say this girl seemed contented, and, as lodging-house landladies go, her mistress seemed a fairly good one; but what a life of exhaustive and unremitting labour, even under these conditions, for a child of thirteen; and what a life of horrors if her mistress had been a brutal or cruel woman! The usual payment is 2s. 6d. a week, but I found in a number of cases the girls only received 1s., or even 9d., their mistresses deducting the rest of their salary for the payment of the clothes which they have been compelled to buy for them on arrival, the little servant being too often in possession of a hat with feathers, a fur boa, and a brass locket, which, with the garments she stands up in, form her entire outfit. A pathetic little story was told me about a bright-faced girl I happened to come across.

"I got to know of her," said my informant, a lady who does much quiet good, and whose name is unknown to newspaper readers, "last year. A friend of mine whose Sunday-school she attended in Deptford asked me to look her up. I happened quite by chance to call in at the coffee-tavern where she was to act as servant, a few moments after she had arrived, and I was told I might go up to the 'bedroom.' Well, I won't go into particulars about that 'bedroom.' It was nearly dark, and I found the poor little soul sitting on the only available piece of furniture in the room—her own little tin hat-box. I shall not easily forget that dazed, bewildered look with which she met me. It was all so strange ; everyone had been too busy to attend to her, and, though she had come from a wretched home, where the playful father had been in the habit of making her a target for his boot shying, still there had been familiar faces round her. She seemed to realise in the sort of way young people do not, as a rule, the intense loneliness of her lot ; and, when I put my arm round her, she clung to me with such sobs that I could hardly help crying too."

Fortunately, sensitive child-servants are tolerably rare, and I am bound to say I failed to find any answering to this description. They were generally what one might describe as decidedly "independent !" One girl— she was barely fifteen —told me she had been in six places.

"Are you so fond of change ?" I asked.

"'Tain't that so much," returned the young lady ; "but I can't put up with 'cheek,' and some o' my missises do go on awful. 'I says : 'Ave yer jaw, and 'ave done with it.'"

This certainly was rather an awful specimen ; but she could not have been very bad, as her present mistress—who, I presume, has not up to the present "cheeked" her— assured me that the girl handed over her 2s. 6d. a week regularly to her mother. This seems to be the usual practice with the girls. Their mothers buy their clothes, and give them a shilling on Bank Holidays and a few pence every week to spend on themselves. A large proportion of these little drudges marry dockers and labourers generally, and, as their training has not been exactly of the kind to render them neat, thrifty housewives, it is perhaps not surprising that their *cuisine* and domestic arrangements altogether leave much to be desired.

There is perhaps no form of entertainment more popular amongst a large class of playgoers than that afforded by the clever acrobat, of whose private life the public has only the vaguest knowledge. The general impression, derived from sensational stories in newspapers and romances, is that the profession of the gymnast is a disreputable one, involving a constant danger of life and limb ; and that young acrobats can only be made proficient in the art by the exercise of severity and cruelty on the part of trainers.

The actual facts are that the owners, or, as they are called, "fathers," of "troupes" are, in a number of cases, respectable householders, who, when not travelling over Europe and America, occupy little villas in the neighbourhood of Brixton and Clapham ; that the danger is immensely exaggerated, particularly in the case of boys, who are always caught when they fall ; and that the training and discipline

ON THE ROPE.

need not be any severer than that employed by a schoolmaster to enforce authority.

"Of course," said a trainer of long experience to me, "I sometimes get an idle boy, just as a schoolmaster gets an idle pupil, and I have my own methods of making him work. But I would lay a heavy wager that even a lazy lad sheds less tears in his training with me than a dull schoolboy

ONE OF THE YOKOHAMA TROUPE.

at a public school. I have never met with a single boy who didn't delight in his dexterity and muscle ; and you will find acrobats as a whole enjoy a higher average of health than any other class."

There are no "Schools of Gymnastics" for training acrobats in London, the regular

general rule, the training commences at seven or eight years old. Many of the children are taken from the very lowest dregs of humanity, and are bound over by their parents to the owner of a troupe for a certain number of years. The "father" undertakes to teach, feed, and clothe the boy, whilst the parents agree not to claim him for a stipulated number of years. A boy is rarely of any good for the first couple of years, and it takes from five to six years to turn out a finished gymnast.

"Is it true," I asked of the head of the celebrated "Yokohama Troupe," "that the bones of the boys are broken whilst young?"

"FULL SPREAD."

"SHOULDER AND LEGS."

method being that the head of each troupe —which usually consists of five or six persons, including one or more members of the family, the acrobatic instinct being strongly hereditary—trains and exhibits his own little company. The earlier a boy begins, of course, the better ; and, as a

Mr. Edwin Bale, who is himself a fine specimen of the healthy trapezist, smiled pityingly at my question, and asked me to come and watch his troupe practise. All gymnasts practise regularly for two hours or more every day. The "Yokohama Troupe" includes three boys, all well-fed looking and healthy, one of them being Edwin, the fifteen-year-old son of Mr. Bale, a strikingly handsome and finely-developed boy, who has been in the profession since he was two.

The first exercise that young boys learn is "shoulder and legs," which is practised assiduously till performed with ease and rapidity. After this comes "splits." This exercise looks as if it ought to be not only uncomfortable but painful ; but a strong proof that it is neither was afforded me involuntarily by one of the little boys. He did it repeatedly for his own benefit when off duty! After this the boy learns "flip-flap," "full-spread," and a number of intricate gymnastics with which the public is.

THROWING KNIVES.

familiar. In all these performances boys are very much in request, partly because they are more popular with the public, and partly because in a variety of these gymnastic exhibitions men are disqualified from taking any part in them owing to their weight. In the figure technically known as "full spread" (shown in illustration), it is essential that the topmost boy shall be slightly made and light in weight; but even under these conditions the strain on the principal "supporter" is enormous. As regards danger, so far as I have been able to learn from a good deal of testimony on the point, there is very little of any kind. The only really dangerous gymnastic turn is the "somersault," which may have serious results, unless done with dexterity and delicacy. There is no doubt that exercise of this kind is beneficial to the boys' health. Several boys in excellent condition, with well-developed muscles and

chests, assured me they were often in the "'orspital" before they became acrobats.

Their improved physique is possibly in a great measure due to the capital feeding they get, it being obviously to the advantage of the "father" to have a robust, rosy-faced company. Master Harris, of the "Yokohama Troupe," informed me that he generally has meat twice a day, a bath every evening (gymnasts are compelled by the nature of their work to keep their skins in good condition by frequent bathing), that Mrs. Bale was as kind to him as his own mother, and that he thought performing "jolly." He further informed me that he got three shillings a week for pocket-money, which was put into the bank for him.

Another boy in the same troupe told me he had over £9 in the bank. Of course, all companies are not so well looked after as the boys in Mr. Bale's troupe; but I have failed to discover a single case where the boys seemed ill-used. Where the troupe travelled about Europe, the lads were exceptionally intelligent, and several of them could talk fair French and German. A really well-equipped acrobat is nearly always sure of work, and can often

BALL EXERCISE.

obtain as much as £30 a week, the usual payment being from £20 to £25 a week. As a rule, the boys remain with the master who has given them their training, and who finds it worth while, when they are grown up, to pay them a good salary. A troupe gets as much as £70 or £80 a day when hired out for fêtes or public enter-tainments. There is one point which will possibly interest the temperance folk, and

which I must not for-get. The boys have constantly before them moderation in the persons of their elders.

"Directly an acrobat takes to drinking," said Mr. Bale, impressively, "he is done for. I rarely take a glass of wine. I can't afford to have my nerves shaky." Alto-gether there are worse methods of earning a livelihood than those of the acrobat ; and, *à propos* of this point, an instructive little story was told me which sentimental, fussy people would do well to note. There was a certain little lad be-longing to a troupe the owner of which had rescued him from the gutter principally out of charity. The boy was slight and delicate-looking, but good feeding and exercise improved him wonder-fully, and he was becoming quite a decent specimen of humanity when some silly people cried out about the cruelty of the late hours, and so on, and insisted that he should be at school all day. The lad, who was well fed, washed, and clothed, was handed back to the care of his parents. He now cer-tainly attends school during the day, but he is running about the gutter every evening, barefooted, selling matches till midnight ! On the subject of ballet

children there is also a great deal of wasted sentiment. All sorts and descriptions of children are employed in theatres, from the respectable tradesman's child to the coster's child in Drury-lane ; but the larger pro-portion are certainly of the very poorest class, and it must be remembered that these children would not be tucked up safely in their little beds, if they were not earning a few badly-wanted shillings ; they would be running about the London streets.

Mr. D'Auban—who has turned out a number of our best dancers, such as Sylvia Grey, Letty Lind, and others—was kind enough to call a rehearsal of his children, who are now performing at the Lyric, Prince of Wales, Drury Lane, and other theatres, so that I was enabled to see a very representative gathering of these useful little bread-winners. Whatever else may

be urged against the employment of children in theatres, there is not the least doubt that danc-ing is a pure pleasure to them. Out of all the little girls I ques-tioned, not a single one would admit that she ever felt " tired." A good many of the children be-long to theatrical families, and have been on the stage since they were babies ; they were distinguished by a calmness and self-pos-session which the other little ones lacked ; but in the matter of danc-ing there was very little difference, and it was difficult to believe that a large proportion of the children now play-ing in "La Cigale," knew nothing about dancing six months ago. Mr. D'Auban has no apprentices, no

FIRST STEPS.

agreements, and no charges, and he says he can make any child of fair intelligence a good dancer in six months. The classes

FINISHING STEPS.

begin in May, and, as soon as it is known that Mr. D'Auban wants children, he is besieged by parents with little maids of all sizes. The School Board only allows them to attend two days a week ; but Mr. D'Auban says : " Everything I teach them once is practised at home and brought back perfect to me." The children wear their ordinary dress, and practising shoes of any kind are allowed. First the positions are mastered, then chassés, pirouettes, and all the rest of the rhythmic and deli- cate movements of which ballets consist.

Many of these graceful little dancers are the real bread - winners of the family. Little Minnie Burley, whose charming dancing in the " Rose and the Ring " will be remembered, though only eleven years old, has for more than a year practically supported herself and her mother by her earnings. The mother suffers from an incurable spinal complaint, and, beyond a little help which she gets from another daughter who is in service, has nothing to live upon but the little one's earnings. During the double performance of the " Rose and the Ring," Minnie earned £1 5s. a week ; now she is earning as a Maypole dancer in " Maid Marian " 12s. a week ; but her en- gagement will soon end, and the poor little maiden, who has the sense and foresight of a woman of thirty, is getting rather anxious.

She is a serious-faced, dark-eyed child, very sensible, very self-possessed, and pas- sionately fond of dancing. Her mother is

devoted to her, and keeps her exquisitely neat. I asked her whether she did not feel a little nervous about the child com- ing home alone every night from the Strand.

"No," said Mrs. Burley, " you see, she comes by 'bus, and she *knows how* to take care of herself—she knows she is not to let anyone talk to her."

Minnie is a type of dozens of other hard- working, modest little girls who are sup- porting themselves, and very often their families, by dancing. As a rule, the mothers fetch the children, or make arrangements for several to come home together. Many of them, whose husbands have been out of work, or who are widows, or deserted, have assured me they could not possibly have got through the winter without the children's earnings, whilst the children themselves are immensely proud of " helping " mother. The pride they take in their parts is also very amusing. One small girl ran after me the whole length of a street. She reached me breathless, saying, " Don't forget I'm *principal* butterfly." Another small

A FIGURE OF PAVANNE

stances an essential, addition to the mother's purse.

Child models, being required almost exclusively in the daytime, are, thanks to the vigilance of the School Board authorities, becoming more and more scarce. The larger number of them comes from "model families," the mother having sat herself, and having from an early age accustomed her children to "sitting." The children of these families have no difficulty in obtaining regular work ; they get a reputation in the painting world, and one artist recommends them to another. In the neighbourhood of Fitzroy-square, Holland-park, and St. John's Wood these families abound, and

AT PLAY.

mite gave me a most crushing reply. She made some allusion to her mother, and I said innocently, "I suppose your mother is a dresser?" She looked daggers at me, and said indignantly, "My mother's a lady wots in the ballet."

The wages of the children range from 6s. to 16s. a week, and, as their engagements often last for four months at a time, it will be seen that their money is a valuable, and in many in-

AT THE LYRIC.

are mostly in very respectable circumstances. A pretty little girl, whose mother is a well-known model, and who has herself figured in several of Millais' pictures, told me with condescension that she had so many engagements she didn't know which artist to go to first.

Mary M——, whose face is familiar to admirers of Miss Kate Greenaway's pictures, is, except for a couple of months in the summer, never out of work. She is a beautiful child of fourteen, the daughter of a cab-driver, who is not always in regular employment ; and, as Mary has a tribe of little brothers, her earnings are of the utmost usefulness. For several months she has been sitting to three artists, and making the

AT TEA.

very respectable sum of £1 10s. a week. In her spare moments Mary takes music lessons, and her great ambition is to become an illustrator in black and white. All her earnings are cheerfully handed over to her mother, who is as careful of her little daughter's welfare as she can be.

"I don't sit as a nude model," Mary said, "but only for my head, and mother doesn't let me go into *any* studio."

As a matter of fact, children are not used as nude models to any great extent ; they do not sit still enough, and their limbs are too thin and unformed to be of much use. Besides the regular professional models, who get 5s. a day, and are pretty sure of engagements, except in the summer, there is a fairly large class of street children who call at the different artists' studios, and are taken on occasionally.

"I get any number," said a well-known artist. "They come down to me, and are kind enough to *suggest* ideas. One small girl said to me the other day, 'Could you do me in a blue dress, sir ; mother says it would go well with my golden 'air.'"

Many artists prefer these children to the regular model, who get a stereotyped expression and artificial poses from long habit. Mr. T. B. Kennington, whose pictures of poor London children are familiar to the public, told me that he always actually paints from the class of children that he depicts on his canvas. The boy who figured in that painful and powerful picture of his, "Widowed and Fatherless," is a real little London waif. His mother is said to have been pitched out of window by her husband, and the boy, whose sad face arrests the attention of the most careless observer, lives with his grandmother, who does washing.

"Do you make the children 'put on' this sad expression ?" I asked Mr. Kennington.

"No, indeed ; my great difficulty is to make them smile, except momentarily. Haven't you ever noticed how very melancholy children look in repose ?"

This may be true about children who are constantly half-starved and ill-treated, but surely it is not true of children in general, or even of the majority of children of the lower classes, who contrive to wear an air of marvellous brightness, in spite of cold, hunger, and even blows. "Sitting" does not seem to be an occupation that commends itself to children, who naturally dislike keeping perfectly still in one position. Nearly all the little models prefer ladies, who keep

them quiet by telling them stories, and bestowing sweets and cakes on them ; whereas male painters have less persuasive methods of making them do what they want. These latter, however, make many attempts to reform the manners and morals of their small models, many of whom, they say, evince an appalling amount of depravity. Mr. F. W. Lawson, who painted some veritable little slum waifs, in his series of pictures called "Children of the Great Cities," told a good little story of one of his attempts in this direction. His model was a small, bright-faced, black-eyed street boy.

"Well, Fred, what have you been doing to-day ?" asks Mr. Lawson. "Playing on Battersea Bridge, sir, and chucking stones at mad old Jimmy," was the reply of the urchin, who then proceeded with much gusto to describe the details of this sport. Mr. Lawson, on learning that mad old Jimmy added blindness to his other infirmities, spoke strongly about the cruelty and cowardice of such an entertainment ; and ended up by telling the story of a heroic deed performed by a blind man. "When I looked up," said Mr. Lawson, "I saw the boy's eyes were full of tears, and I thought to improve the occasion by asking, 'And now, Freddy, what will you do if you meet mad old Jimmy again ?' The little scamp looked up with a wink, and said, chuckling, 'Chuck stones at 'im, sir.'"

Professional models, especially those who have sat to eminent artists, have an exaggerated idea of their comeliness, and they will draw your attention to their good points with much frankness.

"I've got beautiful 'air," said one little girl, modestly pointing to her curly chestnut locks ; whilst a small boy, usually called the "Saint," from having figured in several religious pictures, requested me to observe his "fine froat," as if he had been a prize beast.

In London, owing to the numerous restrictions imposed upon employers, there are only a comparatively small number of children working in factories. Girls of thirteen and upward are employed in confectionery, collar, jam, and match and other factories where skilled labour is not required, whilst small boys are principally found at rope works, foundries, and paper-mills, where their chief business is to attend to the machinery. It is almost impossible to mistake the factory-girl, and even at a glance one notes certain characteristics which distinguish her from her sister workers. Contrast her, for instance, with the theatre child out of Drury-lane. The little actress may be as poor as the Mile-end factory-girl, but in nine cases out of ten she will be very neatly clad, with spotless petticoats and well-made boots and stockings. If you watch her, you will notice she walks gracefully, and instinctively assumes, whenever she can, a picturesque and taking attitude. The little factory-girl is decently enough attired so far as her frock is concerned, but she, or her mother, cares nothing about her boots, which are invariably cheap and untidy, whilst any superfluous coin is

PACKING CHOCOLATE.

devoted to the adornment of her hat, an article of great importance amongst factory-girls—young as well as old. But a still more characteristic feature, which, so far as

PICKING SWEETS.

I know, is peculiar to factory-girls, is their curious method of walking, which is carefully cultivated and imitated by the young ones. It is a sort of side "swing" of the skirts, and has one of the ugliest effects that can be produced, especially when executed by half a dozen young ladies walking abreast on the pavement.

At Messrs. Allen's chocolate and sweet factories, in Mile-end, some two hundred women and girls are employed. Referring to the strike, I asked a highly respectable, intelligent-looking girl why she joined it :

"Well, I don't hardly know," was the candid reply. "It was all done in a rush, and the other girls asked me to come out."

This girl was earning, by the bye, 17s. a week.

The quite young girls are principally employed in packing chocolate into boxes, covering it with silver paper, which operation they perform with great dexterity, labelling, and other easy work of this nature. The rooms are large and well ventilated, and each department is under the care of a forewoman, who not only keeps a sharp look-out on the work, but exercises what control she can over behaviour and conversation. The discipline did not strike me as particularly severe, considering that the girls left their work *en masse*, as soon as one of their number had announced, referring to the artist, "She's takin' Em'ly's likeness." The hours, from 8 to 7, are certainly too long

FLOWER SELLER.

for girls in delicate health ; but the work itself is light, and a capital dining-room is provided on the premises, where the girls can cook their dinners and make themselves tea. Nor are the prospects at all bad. Here is Alice C——, a girl of fourteen, the daughter of a flower carman, not always in work. She is a packer, and gets 6s. a week, which she hands over to her mother. She says she likes doing things with her hands, and would not like to be in service, as then she wouldn't have her Sundays to herself. If she stays on at Messrs. Allen's, her wages will be steadily raised to 18s. a week ; and, if she ultimately becomes a piece-worker, she may make as much as 24s. or 25s. a week. Considering that a good many educated women are teaching in High Schools for salaries of £65 per annum, this is surely not bad.

Of course all factories are not as well managed as these chocolate works, and where the hardship comes in is where hands are turned off at certain periods of the year, or when the work itself, like match-making, is injurious to health.

Still more unfortunate is the lot of some of the little girl workers who assi t their mothers at home in tailoring, button-holing, and dolls'-clothes making. The united work of mother and child yields only a wretched pittance, and, carried on as it is in a room where sleeping, eating, and living go on, is, of all forms of labour, the saddest and most unhealthy. Meals consist of bread and tea, and work is prolonged till midnight by the light of one candle, with the consequence that the children are prematurely aged and diseased. This is the most painful kind of child-labour that I have come across, and would be unbearable, if it were no: ennobled by the touching affection that almost invariably exists between the worn-out mother and her old-woman-wise little daughter.

The lot of the child-vender in the streets would be almost as hard, if it were not, at any rate, healthier. Terrible as are the extremes of weather to which the little flower-girl or newspaper boy is exposed, the life is in the open air, and a hundred times preferable, even if it results in death from exposure, to existence in a foul-smelling garret where consumption works its deadly way slowly. Children find an endless variety of ways of earning a living in the streets. There are the boot-black boys, who form a useful portion of the community ; newspaper boys, of whom the better sort are careful little capitalists, with an immense fund of intelligence and commercial instinct; "job chaps," who hang about railway stations on the chance of earning a few pence in carrying bags ; flower-girls, match-girls, crossing-sweepers, who can make a fair living, if they are industrious ; and lastly, although this enumeration by no means exhausts the list—street prodigies, such as pavement painters and musicians. All Londoners must be familiar with the figure of little Master Sorine, who sits perched up on a high stool diligently painting away at a marine-scape in highly coloured chalks.

This clever little artist of eleven is the principal support of his parents, who do a little in the waste-paper line when there is anything to be done. As a rule, Master Sorine is *finishing* his marine picture or landscape when I pass by, so that I have not had an opportunity of judging of his real ability ; but his mother, who keeps guard over him, assures me that he can draw "anything he has seen "—an assertion which I shall one day test. The little fellow is kept warm by a pan of hot charcoal under his seat, which would seem to suggest rather an unequal distribution of heat. However, he seems to think it is "all right." His artistic efforts are so much appreciated by the multitude that on a " good day " he earns no less than 9s. or 10s., which mounts up to a respectable income, as he " draws in public " three days a week. Master Sorine, however, is exceptionally fortunate, and indeed there is something particularly taking about his little stool, and his little cap, and the business-like air with which he pursues his art studies. Nothing can be said in praise of such " loafing " forms of earning a livelihood as flower-selling, when the unhappy little vender has nothing but a few dead flowers to cover her begging ; or of " sweeping," when the " crossing " of the young gentleman of the broom is often dirtier than the surrounding country. Now and again one comes across industrious, prosperous sweepers, who evince a remarkable amount of acuteness and intelligence. It may have been chance, but each of the three crossing-sweepers I questioned were " unattached," disdained anything in the way of families, and declined to name their residences on the ground that they were " jes' thinkin' o' movin'." This is a very precarious method of earning a livelihood, and is generally supplemented by running errands and hopping in summer. In a wealthy neighbourhood, frequented by several members of Parliament, who were regular customers, a very diligent young sweeper told me he made on an average in winter 2s. 6d. a week ; but he added contemptuously : " Business ain't what it used to be. Neighbour'ood's goin' down, depend on it. I'm thinkin' of turnin' it up." This young gentleman supplemented *his* income by successful racing speculations, obtaining his information about "tips" from his good-natured clients. It seems sad to think how much good material is lost in these smart street boys, whose ability and intelligence could surely be turned to better account. The most satisfactory point—and one which no unprejudiced person can fail to recognise—in connection with the subject of child-labour is that healthy children do not feel it a hardship to work ; and that, therefore, considering, in addition, how materially their earnings add to their own comfort, all legislation in the direction of restriction and prohibition ought to be very carefully considered.

I must express my best thanks to Mr. Redgrave, of the Home Office, for his help in obtaining entrance to factories, and to Mr. Hugh Didcott, the well-known theatrical agent, for his kind services in the matter of acrobats.

MASTER SORINE.

A Night in an Opium Den.

By the Author of "A Dead Man's Diary."

YES, I have smoked opium in Ratcliff Highway, and in the den which was visited by Charles Dickens, and through the pipe which had the honour of making that distinguished novelist sick.

"And did you have lovely dreams? and what were they like?" asks a fair reader.

Yes, I had lovely dreams, and I have no doubt that by the aid of imagination, and a skilful manipulation of De Quincey, I could concoct a fancy picture of opium-smoking and its effects, which might pass for a faithful picture of what really occurred. But, "My Lord and Jury"— to quote the historic words of Mrs. Cluppins, when cross-examined by Serjeant Buzfuz—"My Lord and Jury, I will not deceive you": what those dreams were, I could not for the life of me now describe, for they were too aërial and unsubstantial to be caught and fixed, like hard facts, in words, by any other pen than that of a Coleridge, or a De Quincey. I might as well attempt to convey to you, by means of a clay model, an idea of the prism-fires and rainbow-hues that circle, and change, and chase each other round the pictured sides of that floating fairy-sphere which we call a soap-bubble, as attempt, unassisted, to describe my dreams in words. Hence it is that in this narrative, I have confined myself strictly to the facts of my experiences.

The proprietor of the den which I visited was a Chinaman named Chang, who positively grinned me over from head to foot — not only when I was first made known

to him by the friend who had piloted me to the establishment, but as long as I remained within grinning range. An uninformed onlooker might not unnaturally have concluded that I was stone-deaf and dumb, and that our host was endeavouring to express, by his features, the cordiality he was unable to convey in words. In reply to every casual remark made by my companion, the Chinaman would glance up for a moment at his face, and then turn round to grimace again at me, as though I, and I only, were the subject of their conversation, and he was half afraid I might think he did not take a becoming interest in it. In the few words which I exchanged with him, I found him exceedingly civil, and he

THE PROPRIETOR.

took great pains to explain to me that his wearing no pigtail was attributable, not to his own act and deed, but to the fact that that ornament had been cut off by some person or persons unknown, when he was either drunk or asleep— I could not quite make out which. The deadliest insult which can be offered a Chinaman (so I understood him) is to cut off his pigtail, and it was only when referring to this incident, and to his desire to wreak a terrible vengeance upon the perpetrators, that there was any cessation of his embarrassing smile. The thought of the insult to which he had been subjected, and of his consequent degradation in the eyes of his countrymen, brought so evil a look upon his parchment-coloured features, and caused his small and cunning eyes to twist and turn so horribly, that I was glad to turn the conversation to pleasanter topics, even though it necessitated my being once more fixed by that bland and penetrating smile so peculiarly his own. The smile became more rigid than ever, when I informed him that I was anxious to smoke a pipe of opium. The way in which he turned his face upon me (including the smile, which enveloped and illumined me in its rays) was, for all the world, like the turning-on by a policeman of a bull's-eye lantern. With a final grin which threatened to distort permanently his features, he bade us follow him, and led the way up the most villainously treacherous staircase which it has

A VILLAINOUS STAIRCASE.

ever been my lot to ascend.

" Den " was an appropriate name for the reeking hole to which he conducted us. It was dirty and dark, being lit only by a smoking lamp on the mantel-shelf, and was not much larger than a full-sized cupboard. The walls, which were of a dingy yellow (not unlike the " whites " of the smokers' eyes) were quite bare, with the exception of the one facing the door, on which, incongruously enough, was plastered a coarsely - coloured and hideous print of the crucifixion. The furniture consisted of three raised mattresses, with small tables on which were placed pipes, lamps, and opium.

Huddled or curled up on these mattresses lay two wretched smokers — one of them with the whites, or, I should say, "yellows," of his eyes turned up to the ceiling, and another, whose slumbers we had apparently disturbed, staring about him with a dazed and stupefied air. Something in the look of these men—either the ghastly pallor of their complexion, or the listlessness of their bearing— reminded me not a little of the " white lepers " of Norway. I have seen patients in the hospitals there whose general aspect greatly resembled that of these men, although the skin of the white leper has more of a milky appearance — as if it had been bleached, in fact — than that of the opium-smoker, which is dirtier and more yellow. The remaining occupants of the den, two of whom were Chinamen, were wide awake. The third was a partly naked Malay of decidedly evil aspect, who shrank back on my entrance, and coiled himself up in the recesses of a dark corner, whence he lay furtively watching me, very much in the same way in which the prisoned pythons in a serpent-house watch the visitors who come to tap at the glass of their cages. The Chinamen, however,

friend, watching me narrowly all the time, through the chink between his knees. At this point of my visit, and before I could take any further stock of the surroundings, I was not a little surprised by the entrance

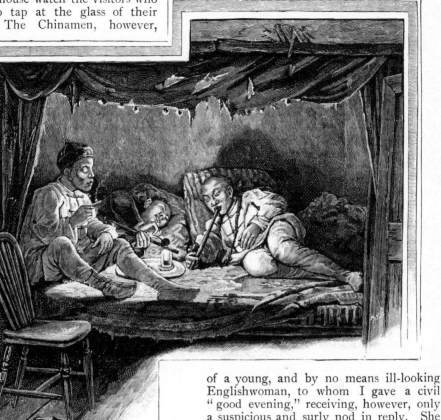

IN THE DEN.

of a young, and by no means ill-looking Englishwoman, to whom I gave a civil " good evening," receiving, however, only a suspicious and surly nod in reply. She occupied herself at first by tickling one of the Chinamen under the armpits, evidently finding no little amusement in the fits of wild, unearthly, and uncontrollable laughter into which he broke, but growing weary of this, she seated herself on the raised mattress where I was located, and proceeded to take stock of her visitor. Beginning at my boots, and travelling up by way of trousers and waistcoat, up to my collar and face, she examined me so critically and searchingly from head to foot that I fancied once or twice I could see the row of figures she was inwardly casting up, and could hear her saying to herself, "Boots and trousers, say, sixty bob ; and watch and chain, a couple of flimsies each ; which, with coat and waistcoat, bring it up to thirty shiners ; which, with a couple of fivers for links, loose cash and studs make about forty quid

seemed pleased to see me ; and, after I had handed my cigar-case to the nearest, begging that he and his friend would help themselves, they became quite companionable. One of them, to my surprise, immediately relinquished the drug which he had been smoking, and began to suck with evident relish at the cigar. The other, after pocketing the weed, lay down on his back with his arms behind his head, and with his legs drawn up to his body, in which singularly graceful and easy attitude he carried on a conversation with his

A MALAY.

and I was swept and borne unresistingly away upon the vast seaward setting tide of sleep.

Of my dreams, as I have already said, I have but the haziest of recollections. I can just recall a sensation of sailing, as on a cloud, amid regions of blue and buoyant ether ; of seeing, through vistas of purple and gold, a scene of sunny seas and shining shores, where, it seemed to me, I beheld the fabled "Blessed Isles," stretching league beyond league afar ; and of peeps of paradisial landscapes that swam up to me as through a world of waters, and then softened and sank away into a blending of beauteous colours, and into a vision of white warm arms and wooing bosoms.

And so we slept on, I and my wretched companions, until, to quote Rossetti :—

Sleep sank them lower than the tide of dreams,
    And their dreams watched them sink, and slid
        away.
Slowly their souls swam up again, through gleams
    Of watered light, and dull drowned waifs of day ;
Till, from some wonder of new woods and streams,
    He woke and wondered more.

Yes, "I woke and wondered more"—woke to wonder where I was, and where were my boots, my hat, and my umbrella ; woke to find the faithless friend, who had promised to guard my slumbers, sleeping peacefully at his post ; and woke with a taste in my mouth which can only be likened to a cross between onions and bad tobacco. And this taste, in conjunction with a splitting headache and a general lowness of spirits, served, for the next day or two, to keep me constantly in remembrance of my visit to the Opium Den in Ratcliff Highway.

—that's *your* figure, young man, as near as I can reckon it."

While this was going on, my host, Mr. Chang, was busily making preparations for my initiatory smoke by sticking small pellets of the opium (a brownish, glue-like substance) upon a pin, and rolling and re-rolling them against the pipe, which is about the size of a small flute, and has a big open bowl with a tiny aperture at the base. Into this aperture the drug-smeared pin is slipped, and the pipe is then held over a lamp, and the fumes of the burning opium inhaled. The occupation is by no means a luxurious one ; for, as surely as I removed the pipe from my lips to indulge in a furtive cough (and it did make me cough a bit at first), it inevitably went out. By means of repeated applications to the lamp, however, I managed to get through the allotted number of pipes, and sank slowly and insensibly into the deep waters of slumber, until at last they closed over my head,

The Home for Lost Dogs.

HE Home for Lost Dogs, near Battersea Park, is a veritable haven of rest for the "lost and strayed." It was started in the most unpretentious way, some thirty years ago, in a back kitchen at Islington; to-day its premises possess ample accommodation for the temporary lodging of over 20,000 wanderers every year; indeed, during 1890, no fewer than 21,593 passed through its gates (homes being found for 3,388), 1,771 were restored to their owners, and 1,617 new homes were provided where satisfactory safeguards were assured. Such are the interesting canine statistics given to us as we start on our tour of inspection, under the guidance of Mr. Matthias Colam, the secretary.

We have entered the great red gates, and stand for a moment upon the threshold of the Receiving House, for a van passes almost at our elbow. Its appearance suggests "police"; at any rate, the driver is an indisputable representative of law and order in mufti. Those familiar cries betray who the inmates are —all sorts and conditions of dogs picked up by the police; this is a deposit of some thirty lost animals about to find apartments for a time. When the muzzling order was first put into force, such a van would have to run over to Battersea three and four times a day, and then leave a load of the lost behind. The conveyance is specially constructed for this purpose. Our friendly "policeman in plain clothes" opens the back door, and there one can see that the interior of the van is made into a tenement of two floors, the bigger dogs being placed below, and the more diminutive species above. Iron rings are arranged round the sides, to which the animals are attached by their chains. A small but important apartment, however, is that placed at the bottom of the van, between the two back wheels. It takes the form of a cage, with iron bars and a grating of fine wire. This is designed for the accommodation of a more than usually troublesome dog, sometimes one that is mad, so that he is carried from the police-station to the "Home" without upsetting the quieter-disposed dispositions of his fellow-animals above.

Of course some dogs are brought here by kind-hearted individuals other than the police, and as many as 500 from all sources have been received in the course of a day. It is impossible to single out one part of London more famous for its "lost" than another—they arrive from the East and from the West. That delightful little King Charles which is just now cuddled up in a corner of the Receiving House has probably strayed from its customary luxuriousness of a drawing-room in Belgravia—it will surely be claimed in a few hours—whilst its next-door neighbour is a bull-dog, with a prodigious head, which strongly suggests pugilism and Whitechapel. The Receiving House is situated on your immediate right. It is the first room into which the lost dog goes when it claims admission to the home. A dozen dogs are waiting to be examined —collies, fox terriers, and two or three nondescripts in addi-

IN THE CAGE.

tion to the tiny King Charles and massive bull-dog already caught sight of. On a beam above, which stretches from one side of the apartment to the other, are hanging the chains and collars of the animals

THE RECEIVING ROOM.

admitted during the past week, under their proper divisions of Monday, Tuesday, Wednesday, and so on. This little collection of a dozen are taken in hand one by one. Should any of them be suffering from rabies, they are at once sent to the "Condemned Cell," to which we shall presently pay a visit. The hon. veterinary surgeon, A. J. Sewell, Esq., is sent for, and if he endorses the opinion of the receiver—himself a man who "knows a dog"—the animal is at once destroyed. Some poor creatures pass a day or two in the Infirmary, and are quickly mended under kind and humane treatment, whilst those dogs who have had their day, and are past all aid, are destroyed.

This Receiving House has been accorded Royal patronage, for amongst what might be called the canine sweepings of London who have found their way here, the Duchess of Teck's dog has looked in ; so has the Marquis of Hartington's, and Lord Brassey's. Amongst the rarest of the wanderers located here have been a couple of African sand dogs, little creatures without a vestige of hair on their bodies, saving a relieving tuft on the head. Even at the Dogs' Home many a romance might be found. Think of a poor lost creature being picked up for a few shillings—for dogs may be purchased

after a certain lapse of time—and then running away with its new owner and winning an important prize at the Brighton show ! More startling still was the case of a bloodhound sold to Mr. Mark Beaufoy, M.P., for a small sum. That dog, once numbered amongst the lost, was destined to become the mother of the champion bloodhound of the world — "Cromwell." Dogs have been sold over and over again and have returned. One little story which we hear as we pass into the main yard is worth repeating. "Bluebeard" was his name, and he was a lively boarhound. All that is known of his early life is that he was found walking about, without visible means of subsistence, in the vicinity of Wandsworth. He was lost—hence, away with him to Battersea. On four separate occasions "Bluebeard" was restored, and every time he found his way back. One night, after the gates were closed, the keeper heard a tap-tap-tap at the entrance. It was the paw of a dog, and when the keeper opened the door it was none other than our old friend "Bluebeard" who had delivered himself up again for the third time. When he crept in he went straight to his former kennel. Eventually, "Bluebeard" was despatched to the country, where, according to the latest reports, he is doing well.

We are now on our way to the kennels— fine, light, airy, and well-built places. We pause just a moment, however, in the playground ; for all the bigger kennels have a playground in the rear, where the dogs are let out to enjoy a merry gambol, or indulge in the luxury of a shower-bath, where at one end of the ground a fountain is playing, under the refreshing sprays of which the dogs delight to run. Wooden boxes are provided under which the animals may go in the summer months, when the sun proves too warm for them, or shelter from the rain during an occasional shower, or inclement weather.

This particular play-ground is inhabited principally by large dogs — retrievers, Scotch collies, greyhounds, and even what are generally known as carriage-dogs. We invite them to the sides of the play-ground— round which substantial iron bars run—and what a noise is there! Yet we are assured that at night not a sound is to be heard—the sudden shriek of the whistle of a passing train over the bridge close at hand, or the warning note of a steam tug on the river never disturbs them. Dogs in company seem to ensure contentment. You may peep into half a dozen other play-grounds, where the creatures will be found to be more of a diminutive type—hundreds of fox-terriers ; indeed, it would seem that the lost terriers number ten times more than any of the other species, whilst retrievers and collies vie with each other for next place on the roll. And round these immense open cages good people wander with distressful countenances in search of those who have left their kennels in the back garden without notice, or wagged their tails

again, makes a frantic effort to pull down the iron bars in its joy, but all to no avail. Then a keeper enters the playground, picks Jack up in his arms, and surely never was a happier recognition. It is really this that those in authority at Battersea depend upon more than anything else, so as to ensure the lost animal being returned to its rightful owner. As a rule, the person losing a dog goes into the yard accompanied by a keeper. He picks out a dog, and it is fastened near the gates, where it can be seen from the office. The owner is invited to this part of the yard, and the keeper watches how the dog and its master meet one another again. This simple plan seldom fails. Furthermore, a set of questions have to be answered by the claimant, and mistakes seldom occur.

It is whilst we are watching the dogs at play, just as Jack—lost no longer—is tripping away merrily over the stones of the yard, that we are entertained with numerous anecdotes by our genial guide. We hear of a devoted owner of a little pet terrier. Hers

THE PLAYGROUND.

for freedom by forsaking the comforts of the hearth-rug in the front parlour. Suddenly a visitor recognises and is recognised.

"Jack, Jack!" the owner cries. Jack jumps up in mad delight, barks and barks

was but an instance of many who come several miles in search of their favourites. This lady travelled some six or seven miles every day for a week in the hopes of having this same little terrier returned to her. It was the last day of the week, and there was the affectionate owner scanning eagerly every dog that entered. At last the rumble of the wheels of the police van was heard, and when the door was opened, there amongst the other inmates lay a tiny creature in the corner fast asleep.

"That's Dot! my little Dot!" cried the lady, and at the sound of her voice the wandering terrier jumped up, and seemed as though it would go mad ere one of the assistants could loosen its chain. Dot went away again with its mistress.

THE KENNELS.

It is needless to say—to put it kindly—that wrongful appropriators of dogs occasionally pay a visit to Battersea, and a capital story is told of one of these gentry who had seen a kind-hearted policeman taking in a lost pug that same morning.

"Good mornin', sir," said this worthy, entering the office; "I've lost my dawg, and if you don't mind, I should feel mich obliged if yer'd let me 'ave a look round the 'ome?"

"What sort of a dog was it?" asked the secretary, coming in at that moment, and recognising the man as a well-known dog stealer. "When did you lose it?"

"This mornin', sir. An' it's a pug, with a collar and studs and a blue ribbin round its neck."

"Quite right—we had such a dog come in this morning," the secretary said. "Just wait a moment—sit down."

Our friend from Whitechapel did, evidently much pleased with his tactics.

In a few moments he was invited to step into the yard, where some four or five pugs were held in check by a keeper.

"Which is yours?" was asked.

"Vy, that's it, sir—that with the collar and blue ribbon round 'is neck. See 'ow 'e knows me!"

When this enterprising gentleman was told that the dog he had chosen had been in the home a fortnight, and, further, that the collar and ribbon had been taken off the real dog's neck and temporarily decorated the throat of another animal, Whitechapel was somewhat abashed, and was glad to get away.

The principal kennels are in the centre of the yard, and are divided into compartments denoting the various days on which the dog entered, so that at the completion of the period which the law requires all dogs should be kept, the animal will have been a temporary tenant of all of them in rotation. The two sexes are separated immediately they enter, and you may walk down the centre avenue enjoying the frolics of the merriest of fox-terriers in one cage, and stay to admire the fine coat of a lost St. Bernard, or pat a good-looking collie on the back as they look almost pitifully towards you. This little army of dogs eat some two tons of biscuits and meal in a fortnight. At six o'clock, when the place is closed, the dogs are bedded down with plenty of clean straw and a liberal supply of sawdust, and every hour a night watchman goes his rounds to see that there is no fighting, and to attend to the Crematorium —the latter one of the most important branches in the work of the institution.

There is just a moment to peep in at a substantial looking shed, specially built for the protection of puppies born at the Home. A magnificent St. Bernard is lying convalescent in the corner. Then, in another part of the yard, more kennels are visited, scrupulously clean, patterns of neatness; and one compartment in the far corner rivets our attention for the moment, for a

The way was pointed out to him, he took a silent view of the road before him, and then, with a sudden bark suggestive that he understood, away the collie went, and delivered the despatch safely as required. This dog is now the property of Major Crabb.

We are now nearing what is, perhaps, the most important part of the Battersea Home, the Infirmary—which is practically the condemned cell—the Lethal Chamber, and the Crematorium. The condemned cell is a huge kennel separated into two compartments, through the iron grating of which often as many as a hundred dogs are to be counted. It should be said that a dog is never put to death unless it is past all cure, and, further, that the means employed are as quick and humane as scientists have yet discovered. For many years the method of killing was by the administration of hydrocyanic acid, but Dr. B. W. Richardson, F.R.S., conclusively proved that the most painless way of causing death was by the use of narcotic vapour, and he superintended the erection of an excellent Lethal Chamber, which was finished in May, 1884, and since then has been in constant use.

It is possible to narcotise as many as a hundred dogs at one time.

"DANGEROUS."

blue enamelled plate bears the significant word "Dangerous." It would not be well at any time to attempt to cultivate the acquaintance of any of its inmates.

The Home has every reason to be proud of its collies. It was a smooth-coated collie borrowed from the Home for Lost Dogs which figured so prominently in the last Military Tournament at the Agricultural Hall. The dog was borrowed for the purpose of testing the value of the German system of sending messages by these useful creatures during the progress of military operations in time of war. The dog was attached to a cyclist who rode the whole length of the hall—over bridges, ruts, and other difficulties in the way—the animal following him. Then the cyclist wrote a message, and tied it round the collie's neck.

THE CONDEMNED CELL.

This generally takes place at night. The unfortunate animals are conveyed from the Condemned Cell to a large cage some ten

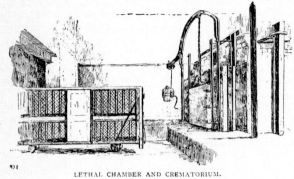

LETHAL CHAMBER AND CREMATORIUM.

feet long, by four feet in depth and width. Two such cages—each of which is divided into tiers—are here. When the dogs are safely secured in the cage, they are taken to the chamber, the door of which is unlocked, the bar-bolt lifted, and the cage with its inmates is run into the Lethal apartment. Here it remains for some six or seven minutes, during which time the chamber is charged with carbonic acid gas, and a spray of chloroform is pumped in, which the dogs immediately inhale. This process of bringing about all that is needed is not strangulation or suffocation, but is essentially a death sleep. There are also two smaller chambers presented to the Home by Dr. Richardson, constructed on simi-

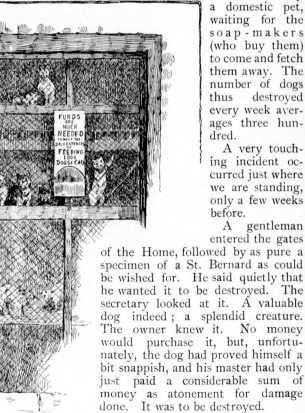

THE CATS' HOUSE.

lar principles, intended for use when a dog has to be destroyed at once.

Exactly opposite the Lethal Chamber is the Crematorium. This is a white brick structure, with a chimney some 65 ft. high. It is so built that the bodies of the dogs do not in any way come in contact with the fuel; the heat being obtained from the coke furnace below. The door of the Crematorium is wound up by the means of a windlass, and the interior reveals a space of about 10 ft. long by 9 ft. in width. After the lapse of some five or six hours from leaving the Lethal Chamber, the animals are put in here. By the morning all that remains of them is a few charred bones, and in a corner of the yard may be seen a dozen or so of sacks, containing all that remains of many a domestic pet, waiting for the soap-makers (who buy them) to come and fetch them away. The number of dogs thus destroyed every week averages three hundred.

A very touching incident occurred just where we are standing, only a few weeks before.

A gentleman entered the gates of the Home, followed by as pure a specimen of a St. Bernard as could be wished for. He said quietly that he wanted it to be destroyed. The secretary looked at it. A valuable dog indeed; a splendid creature. The owner knew it. No money would purchase it, but, unfortunately, the dog had proved himself a bit snappish, and his master had only just paid a considerable sum of money as atonement for damage done. It was to be destroyed.

The master left the dog, and said he would return in an hour's time. He did so, and by this time the creature had been taken to the Lethal Chamber, and lay there on a slab

U U

apparently asleep. It was hard for his master to believe that he was dead. The gentleman even felt the dog's heart to see if it was beating, but there was no sign of movement. Then he broke down ; the strong, stalwart fellow burst into tears as he talked to his favourite. He told the dead creature that they had been companions for ten years, and he felt the parting more than that of a brother.

Again he went away, but the next day found him once more at the gates. He had had no sleep—could he see his dog again ? But it was too late. All that was left of the once envied St. Bernard was a few ashes, and without a word the heart-broken master turned and left the place.

One corner of the premises is particularly interesting, and we look in whilst passing. It is the cats' house. These are in many instances stray cats, picked up in West-end areas, and brought to Battersea by benevolent ladies. They are fed twice a day. In the morning they get new milk, and a varied diet of the customary horse-flesh and fish. Many parcels of fish are sent as presents for the cats. The frolicsome pussies have decidedly comfortable quarters, and they, too, have a playground, in which are planted tree trunks, of which they freely avail themselves. One of the cats' houses is peculiarly noticeable. These are the boarders, for cats may be left here at a charge of 1s. 6d. per week. This little collection in front of us is the property of a lady who has no fewer than a dozen here. All have their pet names, and she frequently comes to feed them herself. These splendid Persians and Angoras—the latter with a marvellous tail—have been residents here for some three years, and amongst them

may be seen a fine specimen of a Russian cat with a wonderful head, which seems to while away its time by curling itself up in its own particular box or sleeping apartment ; and a bob-tail may also be found playing merrily.

As we leave the yard, we look in at the men's reading-room, plentifully supplied with newspapers, and a small library, the shelves of which are principally taken up by volumes of a " doggy " nature. The office, too, must not be forgotten. These rows of immense ledgers contain the records of hundreds of thousands of dogs which have enjoyed the hospitality of the Institution at some time or other. The Board-room is a fine apartment, and round the sides of its walls legacies and donations are chronicled in letters of gold. Framed missives from Royalty may be read in abundance—Her Majesty the Queen, the Prince of Wales, and the Duke of Cambridge are the patrons of the Home. There is recorded in a book at Battersea an expression of opinion, none other than that of Her Majesty, which is worthy of being quoted in these pages. On the occasion of the Queen's Jubilee an address was presented by those interested in the work in connection with this very admirable institution. Her Majesty made reply and said :— " The objects of your association appear to be deserving of the greatest sympathy and commendation ; and your solicitude for the welfare of dogs, the friends of .man, who have shown so much zeal, fidelity, and affection in the service of mankind, is the fitting complement of the charity which strives to comfort and succour the unfor tunate and afflicted members of our own race."

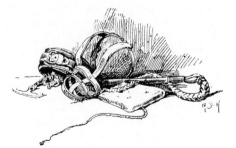

In Leadenhall Market.

By Arthur Morrison.

LEADENHALL MARKET is a changed place since fifteen years ago. Broad arcades and plate-glass fronts stand where stood and tumbled those singular shops in which no man could tell exactly where the main structure of the building left off and the hutches, boxes, boards, benches, and stock began; where the ways were devious and men's elbows brushed as near either side as they may have done any time since the market was founded by good Sir Richard Whittington, in the year of our Lord 1408. Other things have changed beside the shops; by statute of 1533 no beef might here be sold for more than a halfpenny a pound, nor mutton for more than a halfpenny half-farthing. Nowadays this good old law is defied shamelessly.

But the demolition of 1880 left us something. It did not sweep away everything of hutches, boxes, boards, baskets, and smell; thanks be to the Corporation for that they left us Ship Tavern Passage.

Dear old Ship Tavern Passage! Cumbered with cages, boxes, and baskets, littered with straw, sand, and sawdust; filled with barks and yelps, crows and clucks, and the smell of mice and rabbits! What living thing, short of a hippopotamus, have I not bought there in one of those poky little shops, the door to which is a hole, framed round with boxes full of living things, and guarded by tied dogs perpetually attempting to get at each other across the opening. In the days when the attic was devoted to surreptitious guinea-pigs, when white rats escaped from the school desk, and when grown sisters' dislike of mice seemed insane, then was Ship Tavern Passage a dream of delight.

What a delightful door is one such as these to a boy! Here is a box full of pigeons—puffy pouters, neckless and almost headless. On top of this another box full of rabbits—mild-eyed nibblers with tender pink noses, with ears at lop, half-lop, cock, and the rest. On this, again, there are guinea-pigs; and, still higher, a mighty crowing and indignant cock, in a basket.

"FRAMED ROUND WITH BOXES."

What differing emotions do the inscriptions on many boards convey to different minds! "Small reptiles on hand" is an inspiriting

of each may exist together, beaks and claws are ever ready to reach out whenever possible for attack between the bars of cages adjoining.

All the stock isn't kept in crowds, however. It doesn't do. Here is an old tom-cat, for instance, who would scarcely be a safe companion for half a dozen doves, or white mice; a handsome, wicked-looking old chap who won't allow any liberties. And here is another, just as wicked-looking, and not at all handsome. He has begun to despair of anybody ever buying him, and is crusty in consequence of being a drug in the market. It is a noticeable thing that every animal here, always excepting the cats, shows a most intelligent and natural anxiety as to who is to become its owner. They all know that they are here for sale, quite as well as the shopkeeper himself; and every face is anxiously turned toward each new comer, while a rapid estimate is taken of his appearance, dress, manners, disposition, the probable character of his house, and the quantity of table-scraps therein available. All this, as I have said, with the

"A WICKER CAGE."

legend to the schoolboy who keeps green lizards and tame snakes; but his sister, his mother, or his aunt—well, she shudders, and instinctively rubs the palm of *her* hand on her muff. She turns with relief to the milder announcement, " Gentles always in stock," and, sorely misled by the name, wonders why Johnny, instead of nasty lizards, can't keep a dear little, pretty, tame gentle, with soft fur, and trustful brown eyes; afterwards being much edified to find that she has recommended the addition of maggots to the juvenile vivarium.

Nobody knows how well animals of different species may agree together till visiting Leadenhall Market. Here you shall often see hung up in one of those wicker cages, of shape like a haystack, a congeries of cocks and hens, ducks, guinea-pigs, and puppies that shall astonish you by its amiability. They do not fight, being bound together by a bond of common interest—the desire to get out. They cannot fight, if they want to, being packed much too tightly; wherein we see how bodily tribulation and discomfort may bring about moral regeneration and peaceful manners. Indeed, we have here, in these cages and boxes, a number of small nations or states; for, no matter how amicably the inhabitants

"A DRUG IN THE MARKET."

exception of the cats. A cat has too high a sense of his own dignity and worth to betray any such degrading interest in human beings. Therefore he stares calmly and placidly at nothing, giving an occasional lick to a paw, and receiving whatever endearments may be offered from outside with the lofty inattention of a cast ornament. He does this with an idea of enhancing his own value, and of inflaming the mind of the passer-by with un uncontrollable desire to become connected with so exclusive a cat ; quite like the cook on show at a registry office, who lifts her nose and stares straight ahead, to impress the newly arrived lady with the belief that she isn't at all anxious for an engagement, and could scarcely, in any case, condescend so far as to have anything to do with *her*. At the same time, like the cook, the cat is the sharpest listener, and the most observant creature in all this shop, in his own sly way. Watch the casual air with which he turns his head as a stranger passes the shop—to look, of course, at something else altogether, upon which he finally allows his gaze to rest. Note, too, as he gazes on this immaterial something, how his ears lift and open to their widest. The stranger has come about a dog. The ears resume their usual aspect, and the gaze returns to the same far-away nothing as before.

But this unhandsome ruffian has waited so long, and has been disappointed so often, that he shows signs of losing the placidity proper to his nature. Being an unusually good mouser, he has a certain contempt for such cats as have nothing to recommend them but their appearance ; and the natural savagery of

unrecognised genius is aggravated by the sight of white rats and mice across the shop, where he can't reach them and prove his capabilities. So he makes vicious snaps and dabs at boys who poke their fingers between the bars, and will probably swear horribly at the next lady customer who says she doesn't want that horrid-looking beast.

This is not a place where any animal fond of a quiet life would come of its own accord. Here is a most respectable owl, whose ideas of the order of things are seriously outraged by its surroundings. A quiet wing-stretch at night is out of the question, because of the cage ; and any attempt at going to sleep during the day in that whirl of yells, crows, barks, and light is—well, there ! But he has been put high up in the darkest available corner by a considerate tradesman, and makes a shift for forty winks now and again. He is justly indignant at things in general, and meditates upon them in solemn sulkiness in the intervals of his little naps. As the proper centre of the universe, he contemplates the rebellion of its conditions against his comfort with gloomy anger until he falls asleep. Whenever he does this a customer is sure to arrive, and wish to look at something hard by his corner. The dealer extends a match to an adjacent gas-jet, and, with a pop, a great flame springs into being a foot from the owl's beak. Promptly one eye opens, and projects upon that gaslight a glare of puckered indignation. You observe, he never opens but one eye—the eye nearer his object of attention. "Why take unnecessary trouble ? " reflects the sage ; and,

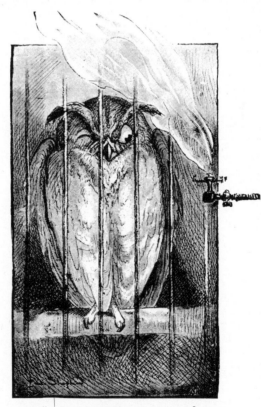

"A GLARE OF PUCKERED INDIGNATION."

sooth to tell, in that one eye is gathered enough of wrath to put out any flame produced by any but the most impudent of gas companies. And though this flame be unaffected, still let us learn from this feathered philosopher, when the world gets out of joint, and all things tempt us to anger—to wink the other eye.

Other birds here, besides the owl, like a quiet life, and don't get it. All such pigeons as lie within boy-reach are among these, as well as some within man-reach. It is notorious that no pigeon can show his points, or even his breed, properly, unless stimulated and prodded thereunto with clucks, whistles, sticks, and fingers. "Bill," says a boy, "look at this'n; tumbler, ain't he?" and he does what he can to make the victim tumble by means of a long lead pencil brought against the legs. "No," observes his companion, sagely, "he's a fantail, only he won't fan"; and thereupon tries a prod with a stick. This failing to produce the desired effect, it seems evident that the luckless bird must be a pouter, so that another prod becomes necessary, to make him pout. But he won't pout, and, as he won't make the least attempt to carry the lead pencil, even when thumped with the stick, obviously he can't be a carrier. The shopkeeper coming out very hurriedly at this stage of the diagnosis, the consultation is promptly removed to some distance off. More pretentious connoisseurs than these contribute an occasional poke, with an idea of getting the bird to show his height; and, altogether, from the retiring pigeon's point of view, Leadenhall Market might be a less exciting place.

But some pigeons are used to excitement,

THE PUBLIC—FROM A PIGEON'S POINT OF VIEW

and no boy who whistles along through the Market is half sharp enough to beat them. Look about you, young and green pigeon-fancier, and see, if, perchance, there be a bird about here which you remember at some time to have loved, bought, and lost—all, perhaps, in a single day. If so, he is probably one of the sort I mean. He lives a gay and fluttering life, staying a day or two with everybody, but always returning to one place. He is what a fancier, careless of his speech, will call a "dead homer," in spite of his being so very much alive and locomotive that human sight, week after week, fails to follow his course. He is a man-of-the-world sort of pigeon, this. Knows his way about London—ay, and any

"A DEAD HOMER."

amount of the country round it—as well as ever did Mr. Sam Weller. He knows people too, and their little ways ; with the number of owners he has had, a very slug must become a knowing card. Look at the innocent old chap. If you be unskilled in avian physiognomy, what more simple and guileless creature could you carry home from here, with the certainty of keeping him obediently with you for ever ? But he who once has owned and lost him sees within the eye of rectitude the wink of absquatulation. The rogue recognises his old buyer again, but makes no sign ; so skilled in human nature is he, and so contemptuous of it, that he allows for the offchance of being bought again, and taken to a place which will revive old memories as well as bring a change of air and diet, and from which the road back is familiar. For there is an owner to whom this otherwise fickle bird is ever true, and from whom nothing short of solitary confinement can keep him, an owner who fully reciprocates his affection, and receives him back after each excursion with a delight which springs from the cornermost depths of his trousers pocket.

"OF UNINVITING ASPECT."

But the chief article of living merchandise here is the dog ; so much so that the customary greeting of the dealers is, "Want to buy a little dawg, sir ?" regardless of the rest of their stock. You observe that they always mention a *little* dog, although dogs of all sizes, kinds, colours, and shapes are here to buy. This may possibly be because just now the fashion largely runs to little dogs—fox-terriers and the like ; but I rather think it is said with a view of conveying, by a wily sophism, an idea of the pecuniary smallness of the suggested transaction—just as a tradesman talks of a "little bill" or a card-sharper of a "little game." Once having engaged the victim by the administration of this fallacy

—well, it only remains to do business with him, the manner of which business it is easy to learn by the practical expedient of buying a dog.

Nervous men do not like buying dogs at Leadenhall Market. "I'll show you the dog to suit you, sir," says the dealer ; "just step this way," that way being into the shop. But at the door of the shop stands, sits, or hangs about on the end of a chain a certain bulldog of uninviting aspect. He isn't demonstrative—never barks or snaps ; he just hangs his mouth and looks at you. It is wonderful to observe the amount of shyness acquired by a man not naturally bashful by the mere help of this dog's presence ; at times it really seems a pity that some of it cannot be made to last. People who have never been known to refuse an invitation before hesitate at that of the dealer ; because, even suppose Cerberus passed, the shrinking visitor must, with all the nonchalance and easy grace possible, walk the gauntlet between two rows of other dogs, straining to get at each other across the avenue, at the further end of which stands the dealer. After which he must be prepared to hear that tne dog to suit him is being kept on the roof of the house, at the other end of many black and crooked stairs, also populated, in unexpected places, with dogs ; and, possibly, after his disastrous chances, moving accidents, and hairbreadth 'scapes, to find that the dog doesn't suit him at all.

Every living creature here knows that it stands for sale, and speculates upon its prospective owner ; that has already been said. Of course, the dogs show it most, and of the dogs the fox-terriers more than any. Come up a side alley, where a window gives light to a bench carrying a dozen. There they sit, ears acock, heads aside, eyes and noses directed intently towards the door. You are standing within two feet of

"WATCHING FOR THE NEXT CUSTOMER."

to know them, you find them to be men of such enterprise and resource that this skipping business is just what they would have done with half a chance. Some keep shops, some help the shopkeepers, and some are free-lances. There is not a dog in the whole world that they will not undertake to get for you, at the right price, at a day's notice; if you were to demand the Dog of Montargis they would undertake to fetch it, even though they were driven to lie about its identity when produced. There is no end to their enterprise, and scarcely any to their number of big pockets. Out of these pockets stick puppies' heads, until the whole creature assumes the appearance of a sort of canine kangaroo broken out in a general eruption of pouches, with young ones in each. They are very good fellows, some of these, as a man with

them, but they don't see you— they are watching for the next customer in at the door. You rap at the window or call; not one takes the trouble even to turn his head. You are not a customer, and it is only with customers that they have business. Personally I don't believe that all this is due to an interest in the visitors; I know the raffish, rat-catching ways of these fox-terriers, and am confident that they have bets among themselves—something in the nature of a sweepstake—as to who will be taken away next. Or perhaps each of these anxious little dogs is straining his eyes, and his chain, and his neck after that master who has been absent for many, many days, and who *must* come back to him soon—who *can't* have deserted him.

Certain men are seen hereabout whom nobody would expect to see anywhere else, and about whom I have a theory. These men are the exceptions that prove the Darwinian doctrine of the evolution of the human species through the monkey. In their descent from the primordial protoplasm they must have boldly skipped all the species between dog and man, so that now they carry as much external affinity to their last quadruped ancestors as other people do to the monkeys. Indeed, when you come

"BUY A LITTLE DAWG, SIR?"

any of the characteristics of a good dog must be, so that I mean no harm when I say that I have seen many a wire muzzle which would fit the features of some of them admirably, were man as unkind to man by police regulation as to dog. And I am convinced that the reason they all wear large coats is to conceal little tails—rudimentary, perhaps, but still tails. This survival from primeval ages is not at all an affliction—on the contrary, a comfort. They quietly wag them when they have "done" a customer rather more than usually brown. This while preserving faces of the severest virtue.

Do they still sell silkworms in Leadenhall Market? I fear not: I miss the signs. In some of the old alleys the privilege was extended to boys of purchasing the eggs — little brown specks spread over a bit of paper—which were kept in a box in a warm place and never came to anything. I must have bought many pints of these eggs; the dealers probably had them in by the peck, for I

"WAITING TO BE BAGGED."

verily believe they were all turnip-seed.

Singing birds are not so numerous here as they used to be—they have migrated, I believe, with a considerable reinforcement from Seven Dials, to Club Row; but an inconvenient and amusing rascal such as a jackdaw or a magpie is easy to find. If any man live a sad life—a life environed with constitutional blues—let him buy a jackdaw. The mere sight of a jackdaw scratching his head, with his leg cocked over behind his wing, is enough to cure a leaden indigestion. But when, after having one wing cut, for the first time he attempts to fly—well, the recollection brings a stitch in the side.

Now and again, during the hunting season, one may see here a fox, waiting to be bought, bagged, and set going before some pack not very far from London, where a find is out of the question. He is an impudent rascal, and will probably be hunted a good many times before encountering a kill. Maybe he has been here before; in that case, he has a poor opinion of human creatures generally, and rather enjoys his situation. He has just run up to town for a day or two, to see a little life, and presently will go back again and take a little exercise with the hounds, to put himself into condition. Then, perhaps, when he tires of country life, he will look up again for a bit, and take a little more dissipation. It's very pleasant, as a change, to live here under cover and be waited upon, but he wouldn't think of staying more than a few days—that would bore him.

A singular property of this place is the improvement effected in the shape, breed, points, and general value of an animal by the atmosphere. If a man take a dog there to sell, he will find that in the opinion of an expert dealer, who ought to know, it is too leggy, poor in the coat, bad in the markings, wrong in the size, out in the curve of the tail, too snipey in the head, outrageous in the ears, and altogether rather dear at a gift. But go in there a day or two afterwards to buy that dog, and you will be astounded to hear of the improvement that so short a sojourn has effected. It has good, clean, stocky legs, a wonderful coat, perfect marks, correct size to a shade, a tail with just the exact sweep, a good, broad head, unequalled ears, and altogether is a preposterous sacrifice at fifteen guineas. Marvellous, isn't it?

Since they are here offered for sale, one

may assume that boys still keep guinea-pigs, although for the advanced boy of to-day such pets may well seem too slow. They are most unintelligent, eat their young, and, so long as plenty of parsley is forthcoming, think very little about their owners. Once having failed to hold one up by the tail till his eyes dropped out, one would expect a boy's interest in these animals to vanish, but a boy's will is the wind's will, and the thoughts of youth are rum, rum thoughts, as Longfellow ought to have said. Wherefore they still keep guinea-pigs. Probably they still keep green lizards and snakes; they used to do so. A friend of mine has to try to earn his living as a barrister, which is a very sad thing. It is all owing to his keeping snakes as a boy, and letting a few of them get adrift in the house of a maiden aunt. She left the premises at a moment's notice, and sold the furniture. This was only funny.

" LIVING MERCHANDISE."

Then she left all her money to a missionary society, and that was serious.

Leadenhall Market, as one used to know it, is going, going; but let us hope it will never be quite gone. Long may the living merchandise resist the inroads of serried ranks of hooks, whereon hang many, many miles of plucked geese and turkeys; birds of no feather flocking together to minister to man's alimentary desires, instead of to his love for those weaker creatures which are so many ages behind him in the tale of evolution, or which have branched off by the way!

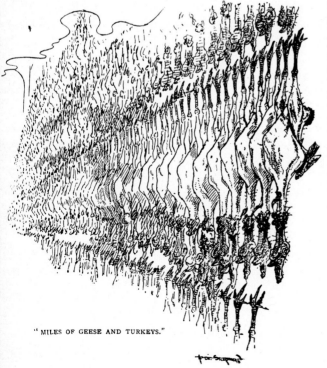

" MILES OF GEESE AND TURKEYS."

A Bohemian Artists' Club.

By Alfred T. Story.

LONDON numbers many societies for artists ; but there is not another so quaint in its style and so characteristic in all its methods as the Langham Sketching Club, or, as it is called in brief parlance, and, in fact, more correctly, " The Langham," for the Sketching Club is in reality only a part of the whole. It is a very modest and retiring body, and does not make much ado, or call public attention to itself by the usual and popular methods of gaining notoriety.

These have always been its leading characteristics. It thought so little of itself, indeed, in the first instance that it allowed itself to be ushered into existence in a lowly shed at the bottom of a mews, or in a stonemason's yard, as some say. This humble abode was situated in Clipstone Street, Fitzroy Square, and the society's nativity took place what time the Sailor King ruled the land, some eight years before Her present Gracious Majesty ascended the throne.

It was started by eight men, who wished by co-operation and emulation to improve themselves and each other in the art which they had adopted as their profession ; and it is significant of the oddity which has ever characterized the society and its proceedings that, no sooner had the resolution been carried confining its membership to the eight founders, than it admitted a ninth. These nine original members were : W. Kidd, F. Cary, J. C. Zeitter, A. M. Huffam, John Knight, William Purser, William Derby, J. Mimpriss, and William Brough, the latter being the honorary secretary.

According to the rules they framed for their governance, the society was to be " for the study of artistic human figures." It was to meet three times a week, in the evening, and work for a couple of hours. Each member on joining was called upon to subscribe ten shillings ; after which, his contribution consisted in paying his share of the expenses. These were totted up at the end of the week, and then and there settled. Fines were imposed for non-attendance, unless the absentee were able to produce good and sufficient reason for his non-appearance ; and for a long time to come the chief business of the committee appears to have been to impose these fines, then remit them, or discuss the means of enforcing their payment upon men who were generally light-hearted, except when weighed down by the lightness of their pockets. Peace be to their souls ! If there were not many Michael Angelos among them, there was an infinite amount of good-fellowship.

The actual date of this simple and democratic constitution was March 9, 1830 ; but it had no sooner been framed than—as in the case of another and more famous constitution—it was found necessary to go to work and tinker it into shape and usability. Hence, between then and now, it has undergone many changes, albeit nothing has been done to detract from its broad fundamental characteristics. The club (for such, in fact, it is) may be said to combine the greatest amount of good-fellowship with the least possible restraint by rule and regulation.

A year after the society's foundation a somewhat radical change took place. It had quickly been found impossible to confine its membership to the original nine founders, and the number was gradually increased to fifteen. Now it was decided to divide the society into members and subscribers ; the former paying a pound a quarter and constituting the governing body ; while the latter paid twenty-seven shillings and had no part whatever in the management—in this also following the example of our national Constitution as it then was.

At first members and subscribers were alike ten in number ; but in course of time the members were increased to fifteen, and a larger proportion of subscribers admitted. This rule still obtains. A still further development took place a month or two later, when it was decided to elect a president, the first gentleman to be accorded the honour being Mr. Knight.

Curiously enough, until this time it had never occurred to the members that their society was without a name. The fact having been accidentally discovered, it was resolved to adopt as style and title, " The Artists' Society for the Study of Historical, Poetic, and Rustic Figures."

From time to time the number of evenings devoted to study was gradually increased, until every week-day evening was occupied. Further developments had in the meantime taken place. In 1841, on the suggestion of William J. Müller, the study of the antique was included in what we may call the curriculum. This involved the renting of another room (the society was still in its mews) at a cost of £25 a year. About the same time the study of the nude was introduced, and became henceforth a leading feature of the society. In 1838 an attempt had been made to form a society for ladies, in conjunction with the Artists' Society, "for the study of costume and the draped figure," but although started with some *éclat*, it appears before long to have ended without regret a brief and forlorn existence.

We soon begin to come across historical names. In 1835 Haydon presents the society with a drawing of "The Gate Beautiful," by Raphael, made by his pupil, C. Landseer. Mr. D. V. Riviere is elected,

From the Picture] JOHN ABSOLON. *[by G. G. Kilburne.*

also a Mr. F. Cruikshank, though he appears never to have attended. Two years later Mr. E. Corbould becomes a subscriber, and in the year following, the well-known watercolourist, Frank W. Topham, and Mr. W. Riviere. In 1839 Dodgson and Lee were elected subscribers; and the same year the veteran Louis Haghe, still living, was made president.

During these early years courses of lectures on various subjects connected with art were given by competent gentlemen. Mr. W. R. Toase, F.L.S., discoursed on "Anatomy," illustrated by living models; Mr. Benjamin R. Green lectured on "Perspective"; Mr. C. H. Smith, on the "Importance of Trifles

in Historical Design"; Mr. George Foggo, on "Pictorial Composition"; and last, though not least, a Mr. R. Cull (one fancies there should have been an "s" to this name), on "Phrenology as Applicable to Art." At that time phrenology was in high favour, was patronized by the great and the learned, and generally regarded as going to do wonders. Many artists in those days, Blake and Linnell among the number, devoted some attention to it; but now, with the exception of one leading Academician, it would be difficult to find any artist who had given so much as a passing glance at the science: if they had, we should at least have been spared the sight of such monstrosities of heads as we now see.

In 1841, under the presidency of John Absolon, another veteran member who is still amongst us, it was decided to elect a certain number of honorary members, and Mr. James R. Planché, the dramatist and authority on costume and heraldry, was the first gentleman chosen. In honour of this election a conversazione was held, to which a number of distinguished guests were invited. This was the first entertainment of the kind given by the society. Since then it has become noted for its gatherings of a similar nature.

At one time the rule was to hold one every quarter. This was when the treasury was in good order. When funds were low it was necessary to be satisfied with two, or even one, a year. They were—and are still—the very simplest of affairs, and Bohemian to the

A CONVERSAZIONE SUPPER.
Drawn by W. H. Pike.

On these occasions the members exhibit their works—sketches that have been done in the class-room, or pictures destined for one or other of the exhibitions — and receive the useful, and generally very generous, criticisms of their friends. Then, to round off the evening, there are singing, music, and recitations, or it may be a bit of character acting. Once we had the pleasure of seeing a well-known A.R.A. and another equally clever artist dress up from the club wardrobe (which is a rich and varied one) as "Black Sall" and "Dusty Jim," and give an improvised dance, to the infinite delight alike of members and guests.

But—to go back a little —in 1842 the most characteristic feature of all in connection with the society had its beginning, namely, the Sketching Club. This is, in reality, quite distinct from the society, although members may belong to it; but its membership is recruited chiefly from outside, and is practically unlimited. The club meets every Friday evening, a subject—or, perhaps, two —is given, and each artist realizes it as best he can. The sketch has to be completed in two hours, and when the time is up, there is a general examination of work, with free criticism, suggestion, and so forth. They may be done in any manner —in oil, water-colours, black and white, or modelled in clay. It is a capital school; every man is put on his mettle, and, of course, does his best. Not a few pictures, now celebrated, had their beginnings on these evenings.

Work being done, supper is discussed; the fare consisting of a cold joint, bread and cheese, with, of course, ale and stout to wash them down. It is at this time that new members are elected. Before a candidate can be chosen he has to submit a sketch. This is carried round by the honorary

last degree. For this reason it is that they are so much enjoyed by those who have the luck to get an invitation. The invariable fare is bread and cheese and salad—*au naturel* —with ale and stout *ad lib.*, or, as a facetious member once put it, *ad lip.* Anything of the nature of ceremony is altogether dispensed with; and as there is always a crush, the feast generally assumes the form of a scramble. City magnates have been known to take part in these *sans façon* regales, and to confess afterwards that they found them more amusing and enjoyable than a Guildhall banquet; while fashionable R.A.'s and A.R.A.'s have been seen to retire into a corner with a hunk of bread and cheese in one hand and a pot of porter in the other, and set to like costers—showing that we are all built much on the same mould, under the clothes.

secretary and shown to each member in turn, his vote for or against the candidate being thus taken.

These suppers are always interesting, and sometimes very amusing, as they can hardly help being when so many men of varied talent, and some of absolute genius, are constantly meeting together and exchanging views. Sometimes, while the others are talking, or "chaffing," one member will be quietly jotting down some characteristic

that will enable you to do it." The suggestion was given with such placid *sangfroid* that it convulsed the room. Keene, however, did not take the hint.

Keene was elected a full member of the society in 1853, though he had already been a subscribing member for several years. He was one of the quietest of men, and seldom had much to say for himself; howbeit, he did occasionally come out with a dry, caustic remark, that told like one of the sly, humorous

Drawn by]   "MUSIC AND SONG."   [*Robt. Sauber.*

faces in his sketch-book, or taking a sly note on his cuff. At other times the fun becomes a little uproarious, and the wildest pranks are indulged in.

On one occasion the late Charles Keene and Mr. Stacy Marks, both of whom were members for many years, had a jumping match. A rod was laid lightly from the rail round which the members work to a box at a height of about three and a half feet from the ground. Marks cleared the rod with ease at a standing jump. Keene, though he tried several times, could not quite accomplish the feat. When he seemed to be on the point of giving up the contest an artist named Wingfield, "a fellow of infinite jest," and a great character to boot, said, very quietly, "Take a pinch of snuff, Mr. Keene;

touches of his pencil; as, for instance, when he bade an old woman who was castigating her ill-mannered donkey, hired for the evening as a model, that she might spare the rod there, as none of them minded his behaviour, because they were not any more thin-skinned than her "moke."

Tenniel, Keene's coadjutor on *Punch*, was president of the society so far back as 1849.

Among other distinguished or notable men who have been, or still are, members, may be mentioned Mr. Poole, R.A., some of whose sketches are as grand as many of his finished pictures are weak. He was a fellow-member with H. B. Pyne and James Müller. The latter was president in 1844, and died during his year of office, killed, as it was thought at the time, by the scant justice done to him by

CHARACTER DANCE BY ARTISTS.
Drawn by J. Finnemore.

the Academy; his works, now so highly esteemed, being invariably "skied." While his pictures now fetch thousands, he died in debt to the society. Alfred Fripp, the water-colour painter, and Fred Goodall became members about the same time. Between 1846 and 1848, Stanfield, junr., W. Goodall, W. Dyce, H. J. Boddington, and A. J. Lewis joined the society, and J. P. Knight, R.A., was elected an honorary member. A little while previously the same honour had been conferred upon Mr. G. Field, the colour manufacturer, and Mr. J. H. Rogers, lecturer on anatomy.

In 1860 the society removed from the quarters it occupied in Clipstone Street to its present abode in the Langham Chambers, Portland Place. Of the men who were then members not many are left, but we may name Charles Cattermole, nephew of the famous George Cattermole, and for many years hon. secretary of the society, and J. A. Fitzgerald, son of Byron's "hoarse" Fitzgerald,* and almost as noted as his father for his histrionic gifts. Several who were then members have since left, notably Mr. Lawlor, the sculptor, the late Vicat Cole, R.A., and F. Weekes. A. J. Stark also was a member at that time. G. Kilburne joined

the society shortly after it removed to Langham Chambers; B. W. Leader, R.A., Henry Telbin, the scene painter, and C. Armitage joined a year later; while between then and 1865, Robert Landells, a man of great ability, who went through the Franco-German War as artist for the *Illustrated London News*, E. T. Coleman, J. T. Watson, F. Lawson, W. M. Wyllie, G. G. Kilburne, E. Law, the engraver, James Gow, and Fred Barnard became members or subscribers. Later, Sir James Linton joined the society, the late Mr. C. B. Birch, A.R.A., and William Linnell, son of the famous Linnell, and himself a distinguished painter.

There is generally, just before "sending-in day," a special conversazione, at which members exhibit their pictures before forwarding them to the Academy to be accepted or rejected. In many cases, of course, this is the only "show" they get; but not a few famous pictures have there been submitted to public criticism for the first time. At one such conversazione Mr. Stacy Marks exhibited his famous "Gargoyle" before it went to the Royal Academy. Mr. Calderon, R.A., thus exhibited his "Coming of Age," and Fred Walker his celebrated "Philip in Church," the picture which was the beginning of his fame. Calderon was a member of the Sketching Club; as was also Mr. Poynter, R.A. Fred Walker was a regular member

* See " English Bards and Scotch Reviewers " :—
 Still must I hear? Shall hoarse Fitzgerald bawl
 His creaking couplets in a tavern hall?

A TWO-HOURS' SKETCH BY CHAS. CATTERMOLE.

cf the society. At one time Mr. W. Gilbert, since become famous in another line of art, was a member, though not for long. He had not yet found his true *forte*, and so was trying his hand with the brush. What he did was chiefly in the comic vein. He was an amusing companion, however, and noted as a *raconteur.*

An amusing story is told in this connection, albeit not of Mr. Gilbert : At one of the Friday night suppers there was present an artist who had been abroad for some time in connection with one of the illustrated papers. He had been half round the world, and was, naturally, expected to have much to say about his travels. But, no ; not a word. " What did you see in China, Mr. Ixe ? What in Japan ? Did you like the Assyrian maidens, or the *Vrows* of Batavia ? " Thus was he questioned on every side. But, like the needy knife-grinder, he had no story to tell. Meanwhile, at the other end of the table was an artist who had that afternoon

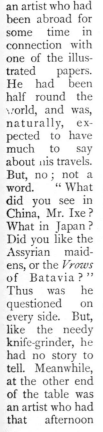

been as far as Bedford Park, and was bursting with adventures. "Fitz could make a better book of travels out of a walk up Hammersmith Broadway than Ixe from a tour round the world," remarked one of the wits of the club.

This is the time to hear from the artists' own lips their varied experiences—often highly amusing—in the pursuit of their profession. One, who has a supreme hatred of dealers, tells how he once had one delivered completely into his hands, *and he did not drown him.* He and three others had taken a walk up the Wharfe to enjoy its beauties, one of them being a dealer. The dealer and another eventually found themselves on the wrong side of the stream, far from a bridge, and it was necessary, in order to avoid a long détour, to wade across. The dealer was no longer young, was unused to the water, except as a beverage, being a teetotaler, and feared all sorts of evils as the result of wetting his feet. He managed to get across in safety, however.

PORTRAIT OF J. D. WINGFIELD.
From the Picture by Carl Haag.

way, do not do as I did, but *put a mop on him."*

It is only needful to begin story-telling in this way to bring out an endless variety. The mention of the Wharfe reminded one man of a deep pool below a waterfall on a northern stream, where he had a most gruesome experience. He had planted his easel, and was beginning to work upon the scene— the waterfall, the black pool, dark surrounding trees, and a blurred and reddening evening sky — when suddenly he perceived a dark object bobbing up and down just in front of the fall. Up and down it danced with the motion of the water, gyrating slowly at the same time. At first he thought it must be a dead dog; then it dawned upon him — and the thought produced an uncanny feeling— that it might be a man's head. Suddenly a stronger wave, a more violent gyration, and there was no longer any doubt. A man's face, with its dead, glassy eyes and streaming hair, was presented to his gaze—and he instantly sprang to his feet and ran, leaving easel, canvas, palette, and brushes to take care of themselves.

Another man tells how, when he was busy upon a choice bit of landscape, a couple of yokels approached, and, after watching for a short time, moved off, remarking that it was a pity such a broad-shouldered fellow could not find something better to do than waste his time like that.

Naturally, there are some stock anecdotes told of fellow-members, which never cease to create a laugh. One hears of the sculptor

"He reached our side of the river all right," continued the narrator; "but as the bank was steep, he had to appeal to me to give him a hand up; and I weakly did so, instead of putting a mop on him. I could easily have done so, the water being quite deep enough to put him out of his misery. But I didn't do it. Of course, I felt considerable chagrin when I had let him escape. Then, to make matters worse, he asked me for some of my whisky: he knew I carried a little in a bottle—'for my stomach's sake.' Naturally, having been so weak as to let him get out of the water, I could not refuse the whisky. And what do you think he did? He washed his feet with it to prevent him catching cold! I implore of you, should it fall to the lot of any of you to have your enemy delivered into your hands in that

One member always raises a hearty laugh by his imitation of a brother member—a man of the greatest good humour, but of third-rate ability—who, debating with another artist on the great Whistler question, thus sums the matter up: "If Whistler is right, then you, and me, and Michael Angelo are all wrong."

Sometimes in this way one may pick up some interesting anecdotes of the men of a past generation. Holland, the famous landscape painter, who was once a member, used to have many anecdotes about Turner. On one occasion he was sitting near to him at dinner, when a lady observed to him that she admired his pictures very much, although she could not say that she understood them. "Don't you wish you had the brains to do so?" replied Turner—a little rudely, it must be confessed.

J. A. FITZGERALD.
Drawn by Robert Sauber.

who, having been too deep in his potations, made his way home late at night with a large codfish under one arm and a lobster under the other, and who found them lying in bed beside him when he awoke in the morning.

Another artist, presumably in a similar condition of benignity, arriving home very late, softly unlocks the street door, goes up stairs, very softly enters his bedroom, and undresses —very softly, so as not to disturb his wife, and finally creeps into bed — likewise very softly and gently; to be startled by his better half asking him— very softly and gently, no doubt—if he is aware that he has got into bed with his top-hat on!

THE LIFE CLASS.
Drawn by W. Douglas Almond.

Members take it in turns to "set" the models, who generally pose for an hour, then take a short rest, and afterwards sit for another hour. They are placed on a raised platform under a top light, the artists being ranged in a semicircle facing them. No one is allowed to speak to the model except the member whose duty it is to set him or her, and the utmost silence is enjoined. Some of the models take great interest in the work of the artists, and like to see what they have made them look like. Many curious characters are found amongst them, and the stories of their humours and oddities are endless and infinitely diverting.

Not the least amusing is that of the man who had posed for apostles and saints so long that he could not be induced to sit for a common coster.

"It would be such a come-down, sir," he said, with a rueful countenance. There is also a story—possibly apocryphal—of a model who had got beyond sitting deploring his changed estate, in that he who had sat for "lords and cardinals" was reduced to "wet-nursing a kangaroo" (having obtained employment at the Zoo).

But perhaps the best story of a model is one that used to be told by Sir Edwin Landseer. It concerned a man named Bishop, a man who will be remembered by nearly all the older generation of artists. Bishop was a bit of a favourite with Landseer, and often sat for him. Once when so

E. C. CLIFFORD (SECRETARY AND LIBRARIAN).
From a Photo. by Scott & Sons, Exeter.

employed he thus addressed the famous animal painter : "Sir Ed'n," said he, " I sees from the papers as you of'n dines with Her Gracious Majesty at Buckingham Palace, and as you gets on very well wi' her. Now, Sir Ed'n, I've been a-thinking—if you wouldn't mind the trouble —you might do me and my misses a very good turn—a very good turn, you might. You know, Sir Ed'n, my misses is a rare good washer, and if, next time you dines with Her Majesty—just when you gets cosy like, arter dinner — if you would just pervail on her to give my misses her washing, it would set us up, it would. Now, Sir Ed'n, you'll pard'n me for a-mentionin' of it, but if you could do that for us, we'd take it very kind-like."

It is not stated whether the request was ever put to Her Majesty.

It would be unpardonable to conclude without making mention of some of the artists who are at present members, many of whose names are doubtless familiar to readers of the illustrated papers and periodicals, or from their pictures in the exhibitions. Among the number may be noted W. Breakspear, Dudley Hardy, Robert Sauber, George C. Haité (president of the Sketching Club), Bernard Evans, J. Finnemore, W. Pike, Edward C. Clifford, and W. Douglas Almond —the last two holding the positions respectively of honorary secretary and curator of the society.

W. DOUGLAS ALMOND (CURATOR).
From a Photo. by Russell & Sons.

All the artists whose drawings have been used to illustrate the above article are members of the Society or of the Sketching Club, or both.

At the Children's Hospital.

CONVALESCENT HOME, HIGHGATE.

 "E want to move Johnny to a place where there are none but children ; a place set up on purpose for sick children ; where the good doctors and nurses pass their lives with children, talk to none but children, touch none but children, comfort and cure none but children."

Who does not remember that chapter in "Our Mutual Friend" in which Charles Dickens described Johnny's removal—with his Noah's Ark and his noble wooden steed —from the care of poor old Betty to that of the Hospital for Sick Children in Great Ormond-street ?   Johnny is dead—he died after bequeathing all his dear possessions, the Noah's Ark, the gallant horse, and the yellow bird, to his little sick neighbour— and his large-hearted creator is dead too ; but the Hospital in Great Ormond-street still exists—in a finer form than Dickens knew it—and still receives sick children to be comforted and cured by its gentle nurses and good doctors.

And this is how the very first Hospital for Children came to be founded. Some fifty years ago, Dr. Charles West, a physician extremely interested in children and their ailments, was walking with a companion along Great Ormond-street. He stopped opposite the stately old mansion known as No. 49, which was then "to let," and said, " There !   That is the future Children's Hospital.   It can be had cheap, I believe, and it is in the midst of a district teeming with poor." The house was known to the Doctor as one with a history. It had been the residence of a great and kindly man — the famous Dr. Richard Mead, Court Physician to Queen Anne and George the First, and it is described by a chronicler of the time as a " splendidly-fitted mansion, with spacious gardens looking out into the fields " of St. Pancras.   Another notable tenant of the mansion was the Rev. Zachary Macaulay, father of Lord Macaulay, and a co-worker with Clarkson and Wilberforce for the abolition of slavery.

Dr. Charles West pushed his project for

turning the house into a hospital for sick children with such effect that a Provisional Committee was formed, which held its first recorded meeting on January 30, 1850, under the presidency of the philanthropic banker Joseph Hoare. As a practical outcome of these and other meetings, the mansion and grounds were bought, and the necessary alterations were made to adapt them for their purpose. A " constitution " also was drawn up—which obtains to this day—and in that it was set down that the object of the Hospital was threefold :—" (1) The Medical and Surgical Treatment of Poor Children ; (2) The Attainment and Diffusion of Knowledge regarding the Diseases of Children ; and (3) The Training of Nurses for Children." So, in the February of 1852—exactly nine-and-thirty years ago—the Hospital for Sick Children was opened, and visitors had displayed to them the curious sight of ailing children lying contentedly in little cots in the splendid apartments still decorated with flowing figures and scrolls of beautiful blue on the ceiling, and bright shepherds and shepherdesses in the panels of the walls— rooms where the beaux and belles of Queen Anne and King George, in wigs and buckle-shoes, in frills and furbelows, had been wont to assemble ; where the kindly Dr. Mead had learnedly discussed with his brethren, and where Zachary Macaulay had presided at many an anti-slavery meeting. It was, indeed, a haunted house that the poor sick children had been carried into— haunted, however, not by hideous spirits of darkness and crime, but by gentle memories of Christian charity and loving-kindness.

For some time poor people were shy of the new hospital. In the first month only eight cots were occupied out of the ten provided, and only twenty-four out-patients were treated. The treatment of these, however, soon told upon the people, and by and by more little patients were brought to the door of the Hospital than could be received. The place steadily grew in usefulness and popularity, so that in five years 1,483 little people occupied its cots, and 39,300 passed through its out-patient department. But by 1858 the hearts of the founders and managers misgave them ; for funds had fallen so low that it was feared the doors of the Hospital must be closed. No doubt the anxious and terrible events of the Crimean War and the Indian Mutiny had done much to divert public attention from the claims of the little folk in 49, Great Ormond-street, but the general tendency of even kindly people to run after new things and then to neglect them had done more. It was then that Charles Dickens stood the true and practical friend of the Hospital. He was appealed to for the magic help of his pen and his voice. He wrote about the sick children, and he spoke for them at the annual dinner of 1858 in a speech so potent to move the heart and to untie the purse-strings that the Hospital managers smiled again ; the number of cots was increased to 44, two additional physicians were appointed, and No. 48 was added to No. 49, Great Ormond-street.

From that date the institution prospered and grew, till, in 1869, Cromwell House, at the top of Highgate-hill (of which more anon) was opened as a Convalescent Branch of the Hospital, and in 1872 the first stone of the present building was laid by the Princess of Wales, in the spacious garden of Number Forty-Nine. The funds, however, were insufficient for the completion of the whole place, and until 1889 the Hospital stood with but one wing. Extraordinary efforts were made to collect money, with the result that last year the new wing was begun on the site of the two " stately mansions " which had been for years the home of the Hospital. With all this increase, and the temptation sometimes to borrow rather than slacken in a good work, the managers have never borrowed nor run into debt. They have steadily believed in the excellent advice which Mr. Micawber made a present of to his young friend Copperfield, " Annual income twenty pounds, annual expenditure nineteen nineteen six : result, happiness. Annual income twenty pounds, annual expenditure twenty pounds ought and six : result, misery " ; and, as a consequence, they are annually dependent on the voluntary contributions of kind-hearted people who are willing to aid them to rescue ailing little children from " the two grim nurses, Poverty and Sickness."

But, in order to be interested in the work of the Hospital and its little charges, there is nothing like a personal visit. One bitterly cold afternoon a little while before Christmas, we kept an appointment with the courteous Secretary, and were by him led past the uniformed porter at the great door, and up the great staircase to the little snuggery of Miss Hicks, the Lady Superintendent. On our way we had glimpses through glass doors into clean, bright wards, which gave a first impression at once cheerful and soothing, heightened by contrast with the heavy black cold that oppressed all life out of doors. By the Secretary we were transferred to the guidance of Miss Hicks, who has done more than can here be told for the prosperity of the Hospital and the completion of the building. She led us again downstairs, to begin our tour of inspection at the very beginning—at the door of the out-patients' department. That is opened at half-past eight every week-day morning, and in troop crowds of poor mothers with children of all ages up to twelve—babies in arms and toddlekins led by the hand. They pass through a kind of turnstile and take their seats in the order of their arrival on rows of benches in a large waiting-room, provided with a stove, a lavatory, and a drinking-fountain, with an attendant nurse and a woman to sell cheap, wholesome buns baked in the Hospital; for they may have to wait all the morning before their turn arrives to go in to the doctor, who sits from nine to twelve seeing and prescribing for child after child; and, if the matter is very serious, sending the poor thing on into the Hospital to occupy one of the cosy cots. All the morning this stream of sad and ailing mothers and children trickles on out of the waiting-room into the presence of the keen-eyed, kindly doctor,

out to the window of the great dispensary (which stretches the whole length of the building) to take up the medicine ordered, on past a little box on the wall, which requests the mothers to "please spare a penny," and so out into the street again. There are two such out-patient departments —one at either end of the great building— and there pass through them in a year between eighteen and nineteen thousand cases, which leave grateful casual pennies in the little wall-box to the respectable amount of £100 a year. It does not need much arithmetic to reckon that that means no less than 24,000 pence.

Leaving that lower region (which is, of course, deserted when we view it in the afternoon) we re-ascend to look at the little in-patients. From the first ward we seek to enter we are admonished by our own senses to turn back. We have barely looked in when the faint, sweet odour of chloroform hanging in the air, the hiss of the antiseptic-spray machine, and the screens placed round a cot inform us that one of the surgeons is conducting an operation. The ward is all hushed in silence, for the children are quick to learn that, when the big, kind-eyed doctor is putting a little comrade to sleep in order to do some clever thing to him to make him well, all must be as quiet as mice. There is no more touch-

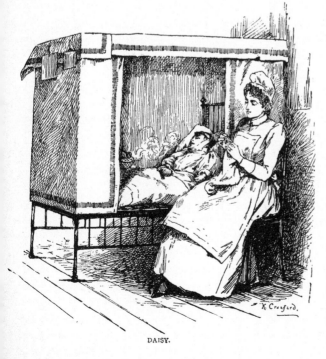

DAISY.

ing evidence of the trust and faith of childhood than the readiness with which these children yield themselves to the influence of chloroform, and surrender themselves without a pang of fear into the careful hands of the doctor. Sometimes, when an examination or an operation is over, there is a little flash of resentment, as in the case of the poor boy who, after having submitted patiently to have his lungs examined, exclaimed to the doctor, "I'll tell my mother you've been a-squeezing of me!"

We cross to the other side and enter the ward called after Queen Victoria. The ward is quiet, for it is one of those set apart for medical cases. Here the poor mites of patients are almost all lying weak and ill. On the left, not far from the door, we come upon a pretty and piteous sight. In a cot roofed and curtained with white, save on one side, lies a little flaxen-haired girl—a mere baby of between two and three—named "Daisy." Her eyes are open, but she does not move when we look at her; she only continues to cuddle to her bosom her brush and comb, from which, the nurse tells us, she resolutely refuses to be parted. She is ill of some kind of growths in the throat, and on the other side of her cot stands a bronchial kettle over a spirit-lamp, thrusting its long nozzle through the white curtain of the cot to moisten and mollify the atmosphere breathed by the little patient. While our artist prepares to make a sketch, we note that the baby's eyes are fixed on the vapours from the kettle, which are curling and writhing, and hovering and melting over her. What does she think of them? Do they suggest to her at all, child though she is, the dimness and evanescence of that human life which she is thus painfully beginning? Does she wonder what it all means—her illness, the curling vapour, and the people near her bed? Poor Daisy! There are scores of children like her here, and tens of thousands out of doors, who suffer thus for the sins of society and the sins of their parents. It is possible to pity her and them without reserve, for they have done nothing to bring these sufferings on themselves. Surely, then, their parents and society owe it to them that all things possible should be done to set them in the way of health.

And much is certainly done in this Hospital for Sick Children. We look round the ward—and what we say of this ward may be understood to apply to all—and note how architectural art and sanitary and medical skill have done their utmost to make this as perfect a place as can be contrived for the recovery of health. The ward is large and lofty, and contains twenty-one cots, half of which are for boys and half for girls. The walls have been built double, with an air space in the midst, for the sake of warming and ventilation. The inner face of the walls is made of glazed bricks of various colours, a pleasant shade of green being the chief. That not only has an agreeable effect, but also ensures that no infection or taint can be retained—and, to make that surety doubly sure, the walls are once a month washed down with disinfectants. Every ward has attached to it, but completely outside and isolated, a small kitchen, a clothes-room, a bath-room, &c. These are against the several corners of the ward, and combine to form the towers which run up in the front and back of the building. Every ward also has a stove with double open fireplace, which serves, not only to warm the room in the ordinary way, but also to burn, so to say, and carry away the vitiated air, and, moreover, to send off warm through the open iron-work surrounding it fresh air which comes through openings in the floor from ventilating shafts communicating with the outer atmosphere. That is what architectural and sanitary art has done for children. And what does not medical and nursing skill do for them? And tender human kindness, which is as nourishing to the ailing little ones as mother's milk? It is small reproach against poor parents to say that seldom do their children know real childish happiness, and cleanliness, and comfort, till they are brought into one of these wards. It is in itself an invigoration to be gently waited upon and fed by sweet, comely young nurses, none of whom is allowed to enter fully upon her duties till she has proved herself fond of children and deft to manage them. And what a delight it must be to have constantly on your bed wonderful picture-books, and on the tray that slides along the top rails of your cot the whole animal creation trooping out of Noah's Ark, armies of tin soldiers, and wonderful woolly dogs with amazing barks concealed in their bowels, or—if you happen to be a girl—dolls, dressed and undressed, of all sorts and sizes! And, lastly, what a contrast is all this space, and light, and pure air—which is never hot and never cold—to the low ceilings and narrow walls, the stuffiness, and the impurity of the poor little homes from which the children come. There, if they are unwell only, they cannot but toss and cry and suffer on their bed, exasperate their hard-worked mother, and drive their home-coming father forth to drown his sorrows in the flowing bowl: here they are wrapped softly in a heavenly calm, ministered to by skilful, tender hands, and spoken to by soft and kindly voices: so that they wonder, and insensibly are soothed and cease to suffer. Until he has been in a children's hospital, no one would guess how thoughtful, and good-tempered, and contented a sick child can be amid his strange surroundings.

But we linger too long in this ward.

With a glance at the chubby, convalescent boy, "Martin," asleep in his arm-chair before the fire—whom we leave our artist companion to sketch—we pass upstairs to another medical ward, which promises to be the liveliest of all; for, as soon as we are

MARTIN.

ushered through the door, a cheery voice rings out from somewhere near the stove:—

"Halloa, man! Ha, ha, ha!"

We are instantly led with a laugh to the owner of the voice, who occupies a cot over against the fire. He is called "Freddy," and he is a merry little chap, with dark hair, and bright twinkling eyes—so young and yet so active that he is tethered by the waist to one of the bars at the head of his bed lest he should fling himself out upon the floor—so young, and yet afflicted with so old a couple of ailments. He is being treated for "chronic asthma and bronchitis." He is a child of the slums; he is by nature strong and merry, and—poor little chap!—he has been brought to this pass merely by a cold steadily and ignorantly neglected. Let us hope that "Freddy" will be cured, and that he will become a sturdy and useful citizen, and keep ever bright the memory of his childish experience of hospital care and tenderness.

Next to "Freddy" is another kind of boy altogether. He has evidently been the pet of his mother at home, as he is the pet of the nurses here. He is sitting up in his cot, playing in a serious, melancholy way

with a set of tea-things. He is very pretty. He has large eyes and a mass of fair curls, and he looks up in a pensive way that makes the nurses call him "Bubbles," after Sir John Millais' well-known picture-poster. He has a knack of saying droll things with an unconscious seriousness which makes them doubly amusing. He is shy, however, and it is difficult to engage him in conversation. We try to wake his friendliness by presenting him with a specimen of a common coin of the realm, but for some time without effect. For several seconds he will bend his powerful mind to nothing but the important matter of finding a receptacle for the coin that will be safe, and that will at the same time constantly exhibit it to his delighted eye. These conditions being at length fulfilled, he condescends to listen to our questions.

Does he like being in the Hospital?

"Yes. But I'm goin' 'ome on Kismas Day. My mother's comin' for me."

We express our pleasure at the news. He looks at us with his large, pensive eyes, and continues in the same low, slow, pensive tone:—

"Will the doctor let me? Eh? Will he let me? I've nearly finished my medicine. Will I have to finish it all?"

We reluctantly utter the opinion that very likely he will have to "finish it all" in order to get well enough to go home. And then after another remark or two we turn away to look at other little patients; but from afar we can see that the child is still deeply pondering the question. Presently we hear the slow, pensive voice call:—

"I say!"

We go to him, and he inquires: "Is Kismas in the shops? Eh? Is there toys and fings?"

We answer that the shops are simply overflowing with Christmas delights, and again we retire; but by and by the slow, pensive voice again calls:—

"I say!"

Again we return, and he says: "Will the doctor come to me on Kismas morning

and say, 'Cheer up, Tommy; you're goin'
'ome to-day?' Will he? Eh?"

Poor little boy! Though the nurses
love him, and though he loves his nurses,
he longs for his mother and the "Kismas"
joys of home. And though he looks so
healthy, and has only turned three years,
he has incipient consumption, and his
"Kismas!" must be spent either here or in
the Convalescent Home on the top of
Highgate-hill.

It is impossible, and needless, to go
round all the little beds; it is a constant
tale of children innocently and cheerfully
bearing the punishment of the neglect,
the mistakes, or the sins of their parents,
or of society. Here is a mere baby suffering from tuberculosis because it has been
underfed; there, and there, and there are
children, boys and girls—girls more frequently—afflicted with chorea, or St. Vitus'
dance, because their weak nerves have
been overwrought, either with fright at
home or in the streets, or with overwork
or punishment at school; and so on, and
so on, runs the sad and weary tale. But,
before we leave the ward, let us note one
bright and fanciful little picture, crowning
evidence of the kindness of the nurses to
the children, and even of their womanly
delight in them. Near the cheerful glow
of one of the faces of the double-faced
stove, in a fairy-like bassinette—a special gift
to the ward—sit "Robin" and "Carrie,"

two babies decked out as an extraordinary
treat in gala array of white frocks and
ribbons. These gala dresses, it must be
chronicled, are bought by the nurses' own
money and made in the nurses' own time
for the particular and Sunday decoration
of their little charges. On the other side
of the stove sits Charlie, a pretty little
fellow, on his bed-sofa.

And so we pass on to the surgical wards;
but it is much the same tale as before.
Only here the children are on the whole
older, livelier, and hungrier. We do not
wish to harrow the feelings of our readers,
so we shall not take them round the cots
to point out the strange and wonderful
operations the surgeons have performed.
We shall but note that the great proportion
of these cases are scrofulous of some order
or other—caries, or strumous disease of the
bones, or something similar; and, finally,
we shall point out one little fellow, helpless
as a dry twig, but bold as a lion, at least if
his words are to be trusted. He has caries,
or decay, of the backbone. He has been
operated upon, and he is compelled to lie
flat on his back always without stirring.
He could not have tackled a black-beetle,
and yet one visitors' day the father of his
neighbour having somehow offended him

CHARLIE, ROBIN, AND CARRIE.

he threatened to throw him "out o' winder," and on another occasion he made his comrades quake by declaring he would "fetch a big gun, and shoot every man-jack of 'em!'" But, for all his Bombastes vein, he is a patient and stoical little chap.

There are here altogether 110 cases in five wards (there will be 200 cots when the new wing is finished), and a few infectious fever and diphtheria cases in an isolated building in the grounds; and the cases treated and nursed in the course of the year average 1,000. But the most obstinate cases, we are told, are now sent to Highgate, to keep company with the convalescents, because of the constant urgency of receiving new patients into Great Ormond-street. To the top of Highgate-hill, therefore, to Cromwell House, we make our way the following afternoon.

Frost and fog hang black and cold over densely-peopled London; but, as we ascend towards Highgate, it brightens, till we reach the top of the hill, where the air is clear, and crisp, and bracing. No finer spot than this could have been chosen within the metropolitan boundary for a convalescent branch of the Children's Hospital.

We are received by Miss Wilson, the Lady Superintendent of Cromwell House, in her cosy little sitting-room; and, before we set out on our round of the wards, we sit and hear her relate some of the legends connected with the noble old house. It is no legend, however, but historical fact, which connects it with the name of Oliver Cromwell. The house was built by Cromwell for his daughter, whom he gave in marriage to General Ireton, and it still bears

EVA.

evidence of the Ireton occupation. About a house so old and associated with so formidable a name, it must needs be there are strange stories. Miss Wilson tells us, for instance, that immediately behind her where she sits is a panel in the wainscot which was once movable, and which admitted to a secret staircase leading down to an underground passage communicating with another old mansion across the way—namely, Lauderdale House, built by an Earl of Lauderdale, and once tenanted by the famous Nell Gwynne. Moreover, Cromwell House contains a veritable skeleton closet, from which a genuine skeleton was taken when the Hospital entered upon occupation. We are promised that we shall see the outside of the closet, but no more; because the door has been nailed up.

So we set out on our round of the wards. It is Thursday, and therefore there is considerable bustle; for on that day regularly come the convalescents from Great Ormond-street. They come to stay for from three to eight weeks, and to run wild in the large garden, and to grow fresh roses on their cheeks, blown by the fresh air of Highgate-hill. The average stay is six weeks, though one or two tedious cases of recovery have been allowed to remain seven months. Difficult cases of scrofula, however, frequently gain admittance to the Sea-Bathing Infirmary at Margate.

The first little ward we enter (all the wards are little here: they contain from ten to a dozen cots) is one of difficult and obstinate cases. But here, by the fireplace, stands convalescent one of these with her nurse—a child named "Eva," stout and ruddy, but with her head tied up. She has had a wonderfully delicate operation performed upon her. She had what the doctors term a "mastoid abscess" pressing upon her brain in the neighbourhood of her ear.

It was within her skull, that is to say, but the surgeon cleverly got at it by piercing behind the ear, and so draining it off through the ear. Some other obstinate "cases" that are well on the way to recovery are sitting about the room in their little arm-chairs, playing with toys or reading story picture-books.

But several obstinate ones are so obstinate that they must stay in bed. Here is one boy who has endured excision of the hip-joint, but who is lively enough to be still interested in the fortunes of the outside world. He has a weight hung from his foot to keep him rigidly extended ; but, as we pass, he begs Miss Wilson to raise him for an instant that he may see the great fire that a comrade by the window has told him is raging across the way. She yields to his appeal, and carefully lifts him in her arms. It is only a big fire of brushwood in Waterlow Park, but he exclaims :—

"Oh ! it's as big as a house, ain't it ? They'd better get the firemen !"

And down he lies again to think how he should like to see the fire-engine come dashing up, and to run helter-skelter after it. Poor boy ! There'll be no more running for him in this world !

Close by him is a very interesting personage, a kind of infant Achilles. That we say, not because of his robust or warlike aspect, but because disease has found him vulnerable only in the heel. He suffers from what the doctors call "oscalsus."

Thus we might go round pointing out that this girl has paraplegia, and that boy empyema ; but these "blessed" words would neither instruct, nor amuse, nor touch the heart. Let us note, however, before we pass on, that here are two champions in their way : the champion stoic, who absolutely enjoys being operated upon, and the champion sufferer—the boy "Cyril "—who has endured almost as many ailments as he has lived months, but who

yet fights them all, with the help of doctor and nurse, patiently and cheerfully.

And so we pass on into the other little wards, and then downstairs into a sitting-room where the greater number of convalescents are assembled.

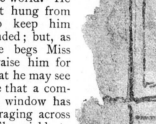

CYRIL.

This room was probably the dining-room of the mansion in Cromwell's days, and here, about the table and the fire where the children sit, must have gathered grave and austere Puritans, and soldiers in clanking jack-boots from among Cromwell's invincible Ironsides. Over the fireplace is still to be seen in complete preservation General Ireton's coat-of-arms, and between the windows are mirrors of the same date. But we have little more than crossed the threshold when all thought of Puritans and Ironsides is banished by a cry not unlike the laugh of a hyena.

Our guide points out to us the utterer of the cry—a little boy sitting up at the head of a couch against the fireplace. He is one

DOTTY AND HARRY.

straight. Over against him, on the couch, sits a Boy of Mystery. He is called "Harry" (there is nothing mysterious about that), but some months ago he swallowed an old copper coin, which he still keeps concealed somewhere in his interior. The doctors are puzzled, but the Boy of Mystery sits unconcerned. With one final glance round and a word to a girl who is reading "The Nursery Alice" to a younger girl, we turn away, and the door closes upon the children.

But we cannot leave them without a final word to our readers. Of all possible forms of charitable work there is surely none better or more hopeful than that which is concerned with children, and especially that which is anxious about the health of children. More than one-third of the annual deaths in London are the unnatural deaths of innocent young folk. "The two grim nurses, Poverty and Sickness," said Dickens in his famous speech, "who bring these children before you, preside over their births, rock their wretched cradles, nail down their little coffins, pile up the earth above their graves." Have we no duty towards them as fellow-citizens? If we pity their hard condition, and admire the patience and fortitude with which they endure suffering, then let us show our pity and our admiration in such practical ways as are open to us.

of the very few children who are afraid of a doctor, and he sees men there so seldom that every man appears to him a doctor: hence his cry. We consider him from afar off, so as not to distress him unduly; and we learn that he is commonly known as "Dotty," partly because he is small and partly because his wits are temporarily somewhat obscured. His chief affliction, however, is that he has curiously crooked feet which the surgeon is trying to set

THE GARDEN ENTRANCE : CROMWELL HOUSE.

Underground London.

[*From Photos. by George Newnes, Limited.*]

IT is a time-honoured saying that, if you want to know anything about this great Metropolis of ours, you must not go to a Londoner in search of information. This is, no doubt, a trite remark, but the more one goes about, and the longer one lives, the more apparent becomes its truth. The foreigner—intelligent or otherwise—who comes to London is very properly inquisitive; he questions, he inquires, he seeks for all that is curious or interesting, with the natural consequence that, after a very few weeks' residence, he can often give points to the man who has lived in the "heart of the Empire" all his life. The average Londoner, on the contrary, is apt to take things very much for granted. He knows that, on the whole, matters affecting his safety and his health are well managed, and, such being the case, he does not bother his head much about the why and the wherefore. The vast organization, the capable administration, the host of details which have to be carefully thought out and rigorously applied—all these things are with the majority of people entirely overlooked. The end is good; why bother about the means? Thus is it that the average Londoner, and not least the travelled Londoner, while he waxes enthusiastic over the wonders he has seen abroad—tells us about the admirable municipal arrangements which prevail in New York, and describes with animation the wonderful catacombs of Paris and Rome—remains in total ignorance of the fact that here, in our great City, he might feast his eyes upon wonders no less remarkable did he but know of their existence. But it is useless to dilate in this vein; the Londoner will not be persuaded to go and see the wonders which lie at his very door. Only through the medium of the ever-inquisitive journalist, always prying about in the dark places of the earth, does he sometimes learn about and admire these native wonders, of the very existence of which he had not hitherto dreamed.

I am bound to admit that, so far as the nether world of the City was concerned, until a short time back I was not much better informed than the generality of my fellows. It is true I knew that there were such places as subways and sewers; but that was about all. I had hardly the faintest conception of what they were like, and probably should have continued to remain in ignorance had it not been for a visit I paid them a few months back. Quite by accident I came across the "Report of the Improvement Committee of proceedings in connection with the Holborn Valley Improvement," which was issued five-and twenty years ago, and desultorily turning over its pages, I was struck by the

A SUBWAY—SHOWING LARGE GAS-PIPE.

A SUBWAY CROSSING.

various references and diagrams in connection with the subways. The thing took my fancy: I discovered how ignorant I was of the underground arrangements which so greatly add to the comfort and safety of those sojourning within the "one square mile"; and I determined, with as little delay as possible, to make good the defect in my education.

So I applied to the City Commissioners of Sewers for the necessary authority, and right willingly was it accorded. The Chairman, Mr. H. G. Smallman, entered enthusiastically into the matter, remarking that if the thing was going to be done at all, it should be done thoroughly. Remember, this was the very first time that it had been pro-

LADDERS CONNECTING SUBWAYS OF DIFFERENT LEVELS.

posed to write an illustrated article on the subject. The Chairman was rather dubious as to whether we should be able to get any satisfactory photographs of the sewers; but at all events, he expressed his willingness to do all he could to help us. So that we started on our task under the best of auspices.

Behold us, then, one September afternoon assembled outside the large iron gate beneath Holborn Viaduct— that gate which most people have noticed, but the purpose for which it is used known to very few. Besides the Chairman, there were Captain Robert Gresley Hall, D.I.., the Chairman of the Streets Committee; Mr. D. G. Ross, the City Engineer; and Mr. H. Montague Bates, the Chief Clerk to the Commissioners, who, according to Mr. Smallman, is virtually the "permanent chairman." The photographer, with his assistant and the writer, brought our little party up to eight all told. When the gate opened at our summons, Mr. W. J. Liberty, the City Inspector of Subways and—under the Engineer — head of all practical matters appertaining to them, was waiting to show us over his territory. The iron gate, through which the sunlight was streaming, closed with a clang, and walking up two or three stairs, we set out along one of the thoroughfares of the underground city.

In the first instance, I experienced a feeling of disappointment. The reality was so different from what I had expected. My idea had

A NARROW SUBWAY OVER THE L. C. AND D. RAILWAY.

been that a subway would prove as Mr. Mantalini might have said, a "demnition deuced damp," sort of a place, smelling of the earth, dark and filled with an atmosphere resembling that of a charnel-house. And what did I see? A long, clean, and well garnished looking passage, dimly illumined by gas-jets (which, by the way, were specially provided for our visit), and having an atmosphere almost as healthy as that we had just left. But the feeling of disappointment soon gave way to one of admiration when we walked along the subway, and the uses of the various pipes which ran along one side were pointed out to me. They include the mains of the Gas, New River, Hydraulic Power, and Electric Light Companies, also the

SUBWAY UNDER PRINCE CONSORT'S STATUE.

UNDER THE GREAT FIRE OF 1897, SHOWING THE MAINS WHICH SUPPLIED WATER TO THE FIRE-ENGINES.

gency or fire, all that has to be done is to cut off the service at the particular branch where the mischief has occurred. As we went along, the Superintendent explained to me the exceedingly ingenious manner in which the difficulties incidental to the construction of the subways had been surmounted, and also pointed out how they were ventilated and generally kept sweet and clean. But as this is not a technical article, I need not weary the reader with such details, interesting as they are to those with a knowledge of underground engineering. Perhaps the most interesting subway of them all is the length on the southern side of Holborn, between Farringdon Street and Shoe Lane, which is lighted by gratings, filled with glass lenses, placed at intervals of 40ft. These render it sufficiently light by day for the purposes of inspection and work. The only daylight which gets into the others comes through the ventilating gratings in the footway, and this has to be supplemented by artificial light. It might be thought, in view of the possibility of leakage from the gas mains, that working in the subways might not be unattended by danger. The idea certainly struck me, and I speedily inquired of the Superintendent whether it was safe to smoke. His answer speedily reassured me. Every morning, before any work is done, a most complete inspection is made; armed with "Davys," the Superintendent and some of his men

pneumatic tubes and hundreds of wires belonging to the G.P.O.; and the arrangements whereby the service mains are connected to the various houses show that simplicity which constitutes the high-water mark of mechanical ingenuity. The usual time for making the connection is half an hour, and in case of non-payment of rates, a house can be cut off from its gas, water, electric light, or power supply in a few minutes, and this, moreover, without the unfortunate tenant or the general public knowing anything about it.

I was rather amused to notice that the names of the various streets under which we were passing were posted upon the walls, as were also the numbers of the houses served by the mains. Thus, in case of emer-

SUBWAY UNDER THE BANK AND G.P.O.

make a complete tour of the subways, testing doubtful-looking places, and if anything wrong be discovered, speedily setting it to rights. And be sure an extra inspection is made before the arrival of any distinguished visitors.

Presently, I was astonished to learn that we actually stood over the London, Chatham, and Dover Railway ! There we were, after painfully making our way through a subway which necessitated our walking bent double, in order to avoid striking our heads against the girders, directly above Snow Hill Station. Yes, there is no doubt about it. As we wait we can distinctly hear a train come in and the porters calling out its destination. It seems exceedingly close, but closer still, above us, we can hear the footsteps of the people on the pavement in Snow Hill. It is rather uncanny this, and especially so when one learns that only 6in. separates us from the street above and only a bare ¼in. of iron girder (for we are literally *in* a girder) prevents us from falling some 40ft. on to the metals ! It is a novel experience (especially when the train is moving below, and the spot in which we stand is positively vibrating !), and we are glad to have had it, but everyone is obviously concerned in trying not to allow his sigh of relief to

DESCENDING FROM A VESTIBULE.

become too apparent when we resume our journey. If anyone looks pale, it must, of course, be attributed to the cramped position in which we have been standing !

Shortly afterwards we arrived at a spot which, we were informed, was immediately under the Prince Consort's statue at Holborn Circus.

Coming back to the Superintendent's office, I was shown a great number of coins nailed to the counter. These, I was told, came through the gratings placed at intervals for ventilating purposes. It appears that gentlemen who make a business of passing spurious coin sometimes find it necessary to get rid of their stock-in-trade with the utmost despatch ; they drop the coins through the gratings under the impression that they will fall into the sewers and be effectually lost. Alas ! for the guilty one's hopes, the coins are found shining on the clean stone floor of the subway, and go to swell the stock in the superintendent's office. I asked him whether other articles were ever found. He replied : "Yes, we get plenty of empty purses. This is what the light-fingered gentry do. They take them from the pockets, or so-called 'pockets,' of ladies, and after carefully emptying them, drop them down the shafts.

ENTRANCE IN SHOE LANE TO THE SUBWAY SEWERS.

scientific men, engineers, and sanitarians from Brazil, Malta, San Francisco, Finland, Santiago, Cologne, Copenhagen, Sydney, and, in fact, almost every great city, have visited the subways. And in nearly every instance the visitor has written a few words expressing his surprise and admiration at what he has seen. I could have stayed a long time chatting to the Superintendent, but the shadows were already beginning to draw in, and it was time for us to start upon the second half of our journey.

First he took me to the subway sewers which lie under Holborn Viaduct. These sewers are quite unique in their way. As nearly as possible they follow the natural slope of the ground as it descended originally from the hills to the level of Farringdon Street, and consequently between the underside of the subways and the sewer is a large space, and the effect, when looking up from the latter, is very striking. Standing in the sewer (by the way, one is able to traverse these sewers dry-shod, a platform running along one side) one seems to be in a lofty vault. It is, of course, pitch dark, for even the glimmer of light coming through the gratings in the roadway which relieve the murkiness of the ordinary sewers is absent here. The space under the road in Farringdon Street is utilized for business purposes, large cellars having been constructed, with which communication can easily be made from the houses in the vicinity. These sewers are ventilated by square openings and

A STAIRWAY DESCENT.

We find most of these in the dark days of winter, and chiefly in the neighbourhood of crowded Smithfield. I seldom find a gentleman's purse; they mostly belong to City work-girls. The professional thieves know that when these girls draw their scanty wages on Saturday, they usually go to the great markets at Smithfield to make their little purchases, and ply their nefarious trade accordingly."

Another interesting object in the Superintendent's little room is the " Visitors' Book." In it the names of foreign visitors predominate ; during the last year or so,

SUBWAY SEWER—HOLBORN CIRCUS.

SUBWAY SEWER—SHOWING GROWTH OF FUNGUS.

this was our objective. Quite a crowd assembled to witness our descent ; so large, indeed, was it that the kindly offices of two constables had to be requisitioned to enable us to get through. Many and diverse were the surmises with regard to our object. In spite of the fact that we were all smoking cigars, it never seemed to occur to any of the spectators that we were not the ordinary sewermen. Most of the bystanders thought something was wrong ; this opinion rapidly gained ground, and in a few seconds it was freely whispered around that we were a " rescue party " going to succour some poor fellow who had been overpowered by the noxious fumes down below !

I am afraid, judging by the gingerly

shafts, and receive all the drainage from the houses on the Viaduct. Very great care and ingenuity have been exercised in the construction of these sewers, and also in the disposal of the gas, water, and telegraph pipes in the subways ; in fact, everything is so easy of access that it is thought that only under the most exceptional circumstances will it ever be necessary to open up the roadway, and thus cause a hindrance to traffic and stoppage of business.

Before going down into the ordinary sewers it was necessary for us to equip ourselves. First off came our boots, and over our socks and trousers went thick woollen stockings, and over these huge waterproof boots reaching to the thighs. The upper part of the body was covered with a rough blue smock, very similar to those worn by the coastguardsmen. In fact, there was something altogether nautical about the whole rig-out, the resemblance being heightened by the oilskin " sou'-westers " we wore on our heads. We were also provided with rough gloves, as we had to seize hold of things not very pleasant to the touch. Curious looking objects we were when fully dressed, although in one or two cases, which need not be particularized, the effect was decidedly becoming.

When all were ready, out we sallied into Farringdon Street. About 100yds. from the Viaduct is one of the familiar iron plates let into the pavement, and

ORDINARY SEWER IN COURSE OF CONSTRUCTION.

manner in which we went down the shaft, that we should not have been much good had any great difficulties been encountered. It was a primitive sort of ladder we had to go down, merely consisting of iron rings driven into the wall at intervals, and in our cumbrous and unaccustomed attire it was not a very comfortable job. However, we got down without any casualties, and, arrived at the bottom, found one of the sewermen waiting for us. He provided us each with a wooden sconce holding a candle, and thus provided we went along a short, sloping passage, at the end of which stood another guide, who assisted us to step down into the sewer itself.

NATURAL CAVE, THROUGH WHICH BUCKLERSBURY SEWER IS CUT.

Down each one of us stepped into about a foot of swiftly flowing water ; the Superintendent of the Sewers, accompanied by some of his men, placed himself at our head, and in single file we commenced our novel march.

I looked around me curiously. Down here the contrast presented with the clean and cheerful-looking subways was very great. Not, however, that there was anything particularly offensive about the sewers. The air, though close and hot, was not offensive, and there was little or no odour in the large main. But from my position in rear of our party, I could not help but be struck by the weird picturesqueness of the scene. The pitchy darkness of the arched passage in which we stood was dimly lighted up for a few yards around by our candles as we passed along, and the lights and shadows danced and flickered up the walls and along the surface of the water like veritable Will-o'-the-Wisps. Far ahead another beam of light—light of a whiter and more translucent character than that shed by our candles—shone steadily across the channel. It neither flickered nor wavered, but in the distance, sharply outlined against the grim background, looked like a piece of wide tape drawn tightly from wall to wall and just resting upon the surface of the water. As we approached it seemed to broaden out and its edges grew less sharply defined ; the blacks and whites began to run into one another until, when we got close up to it, it expanded and diffused itself all around us, and we saw that the little beam we had seen from a distance really came from Nature's own magic-lantern—was, in fact, neither more nor less than the afternoon sunlight finding its way through the narrow interstices of a grating! Why had we no great "impressionist" in our party, someone blessed with the seeing eye and the cunning hand to have seized upon that picture, to have retained it, and finally to have reproduced it as a marvellous study in blacks and whites? Certainly, no sun-lit ocean, no fog-enveloped city, no mist-laden stream could have furnished more

FLUSHING GATE OF ORDINARY SEWER.

fitting subject for a great painter than this beam of light in a City sewer.

On we went, our progress necessarily slow, for the bottom was slippery, and the stream ran swiftly past our legs. My guide explained that when there was a heavy downpour of rain outside, the word was given, and the men all went up to the surface, for the rush of surface-water filled the main almost up to the roof, and the augmented stream came sweeping along with the rush and roar of a mountain torrent. "No," he said, "we don't have accidents; we can't afford to. If a man once got caught in such a torrent, there'd be no saving him, unless the water happened to be lower at a junction, and he managed to

One of the sewermen was requested to bend down; upon his sturdy shoulders the apparatus was placed; then we all waited patiently until the magnesium wire flashed out and made us all blink. Whether the picture was a success or not may be left to the reader to say. Possibly the subjects are not looking very well pleased, but when you are standing in a stream of running water, and can feel yourself perspiring profusely under a lot of unaccustomed garments; while, moreover, the temperature is some twenty or thirty degrees higher than would be comfortable, and your eyes are getting a little strained by the curious half-light, it is by no means the easiest of tasks to obey the photo-

GROUP OF COMMISSIONERS AND AUTHOR, IN THE OLD FLEET SEWER.

regain his foothold, otherwise he'd be carried along with the stream until it discharged itself in the river at Barking. That's where he'd be found ; at least, what was left of him."

The water, as I have said, was only from 1ft. to 18in. deep, but after this little conversation I found myself taking particular care as to how and where I put my feet down. Presently the photographer ordered us to halt and arrange ourselves. He wanted to take a group. Then a difficulty arose : his camera would rest upon its stand, but where was he to find a support for his flash-light apparatus ? Happy thought—a human stand !

grapher's stereotyped command to "look pleasant." Our photographer, however, was a man of sense; he did not waste unnecessary time in giving us minute instructions how to deport ourselves, but having once got us focused, "took us" without further ado.

After being photographed, some of the party seemed disinclined to go much farther. So, leaving them in the broad main, the Superintendent, at my request, took me to some of the side-streets and by-ways of the underground city. As we went, I seized the opportunity of questioning him upon his occupation. He seemed to think it was healthy enough.

" Oh, yes, men get knocked up sometimes, but it's more often through catching colds than anything else. You see, it's hot down here, and if men loiter about up above, especially in the cold weather, they're likely to get chills. No, we don't often have men on the sick list with fevers or anything of that sort. Why should we? Its healthy enough down here; you yourself can testify that the smell is no worse than that you often encounter in the open street. Now and again, of course, when at a bend or narrow passage, there's an accumulation of sewage, and the stream gets partially dammed, the men have a rather unpleasant job to perform; but as a rule the work is not so objectionable as you would imagine. Yes, sometimes a man will stay down here for six or seven hours at a stretch, and they seem none the worse. Smoke? Yes, as you see" (pointing to his pipe), "I smoke, and so do most of my men; possibly, if we didn't, the smells which we *sometimes* meet with might affect us more."

We entered one of the branches, and conversation, except of the most limited description, became impossible. The roof was so low that we had to bend almost double to avoid damaging ourselves; added to this, it was constructed on a sharpish incline, and the bottom being slippery, it was necessary to proceed with caution. As my guide explained, had it been a wet day this branch would have been quite unnegotiable; as it was, the water in it was only a few inches deep. This came from the surface, as I very soon saw, for at the top end was one of the gulleys covered with an iron grating, to be seen in the roadway.

Back we went as we had come; past the place where the main stream forks out into two branches, in which the current, of course, flows more slowly. Along one of these we went, then up another branch even smaller than the first and more difficult, for here the water was almost knee-deep, and was swirling and eddying like the river around the buttresses of one of the great bridges. Previously I had mentioned to my guide that if possible I should like to get a glimpse of some of the rats with which the sewers abound. He had explained that, though they came out more freely at night, he might manage to show me a few in one of the less-frequented portions of the sewers. And this was the place he had chosen.

Painfully we made our way for some forty or fifty yards, and then, posting ourselves in a niche in the wall, we waited, but ne'er a rat did we see. Rather disappointed, we were just turning to go back, when I fancied I saw a dark shape flit past our feet. It may have been a rat or merely a shadow; at all events, I started and nearly lost my balance. With a clutch at my companion, I regained it; then, as I stood upright, found we were in total darkness. As I slipped, my sconce fell from my hand, and was now being gaily borne eastward at the rate of two or three miles an hour, and, in grabbing at the Superintendent, I had inadvertently extinguished his candle; and we had not a match between us! The only thing to do was to grope our way back in the dark. Luckily, my companion could have found his way about blindfold, and consequently laughed heartily at our predicament. He led the way, and I followed, touching him lightly every few yards to make sure I was in his tracks, as the darkness was so intense that I could scarcely distinguish him. Now, I have a curious fact to relate. The Superintendent declares it was my imagination, but at the time I could have sworn that though never a rat made his appearance when, with candles lit, we stood on the look-out, they simply came out in shoals and rioted about our feet when we were journeying slowly and painfully in the dark. Well, it may have been imagination, and perhaps the journey in the dark had played upon my nerves more than I cared to own.

When we rejoined the rest of the party, they were all waiting and wondering what had become of us. They laughed heartily when we told our story, and frankly expressed their incredulity when I spoke about the rats. But they expressed no inclination to go and find out for themselves.

And so back we all went to the shaft, and one by one climbed our way to the surface. And how glad were we to get there! It was an exceedingly interesting experience, and one that it falls to the lot of few to have, and that I think all of us fully recognised. But after a couple of hours in the nether world, it was doubly delightful to feel the fresh breeze blowing on our cheeks, to hear the busy hum and clatter of the traffic, and to see once again the glorious blue sky over our heads.

Street-Corner Men.

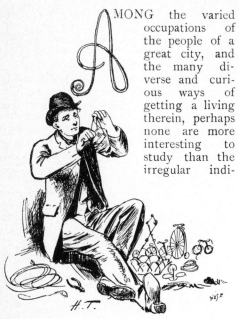

AMONG the varied occupations of the people of a great city, and the many diverse and curious ways of getting a living therein, perhaps none are more interesting to study than the irregular indi-viduals who may be seen at various street corners, and almost on any night of the week, in the various High streets and main thoroughfares of the suburbs, cajoling, lecturing, flattering, preaching, and dogmatically and assertively declaring, by all and every kind of method, the advantages to the public of an invest-ment in their particular kind of goods or a subscription towards the open-air entertain-ment they provide. The copper wire-worker, who with aid of pliers rapidly evolves models of bicycles, ordinaries and safeties, flower-stands, vases, card-baskets, &c.; the glass collar-stud and inexhaustible glass fountain-pen seller; the little old man who, with candle and old kettle, constantly pierces holes in the latter to mend with his patent solder, "Two sticks a penny, any child can do it"; the public benefactor and proprietor of a patent corn solvent; the con-juring-cards seller, "any one, man, woman, or child, can perform these ere tricks the same has wot hi do"; the boot-blacking stall-keeper; the silverer of old brass articles; the herb-vendor of penny packets to mix with tobacco to destroy the ill effects of nicotine, with printed placard of illustrious person-ages' opinions of smoking; the purveyor of old monthly parts of various illustrated magazines and periodicals, the umbrella seller, the conjuror, the open-air reciter; these and many others, with every kind of dodge and manœuvre to extract pence from the pockets of the people, are the street-corner men of this great metropolis.

A curious fact about these itinerants is observable; the majority are selling medi-cines or compounds to cure the ills of the flesh, presumably the needs and necessities of the people in the direction of cheap medicines receiving more attention, and the trade being more lucrative, than the retail-ing of articles of a domestic character. Their methods of attracting attention are various. One well-known character about the London streets regularly prefaces the sale of his patent digestive cure-all, kill-pain, stomach-regulating tonic with a rather elaborate experiment with two wine-glasses, apparently clean and empty, somewhat on the lines of the conjuror's manipulation of a variety of drinks.

A little cold water poured into one makes no change, but with the other a muddy, dirty-red coloured liquid is the result, typical of a disordered state of health.

"TWO STICKS A PENNY."

"OLD MONTHLY PARTS."

"The idea then struck me," he continues, "that I would never rest until, unaided and alone, I had become the greatest doctor of the London streets. That proud position I now enjoy. 'How do you do if, Shaw?' says one. 'Mere luck,' says another. How have I done it? I will tell you how I have done it. Take my health-giving hop-bitters; not Dr. Soules' hop-bitters, for which you have to pay 1s. 1½d. and

"Now," triumphantly declares the street quack, "you will see the magical effect of my patent curative, blood purifying, health-restoring, digestive tonic." Two drops of this into the muddy, dirty-red liquid chemically restores the water to its former apparent purity, and the effect upon the health of the purchaser is analogously equally efficacious. Strong lungs, a tremendous voice, and emphatic declarations help to sell a great number of bottles.

Another regenerator of his race begins from the platform of a smart pony and trap, by an amusing account of having landed from New York with the traditional half-crown in his pocket, and, wandering down the Whitechapel-road, was attracted by a quack medicine-vendor.

2s. 7½d. a bottle, but take my patent hop-bitters, one penny a packet, and you will never again be troubled—," and here follows a splendid list of every ailment that could possibly afflict suffering humanity. Having sold out all his hop-bitters, he would then bring on the scene, utterly and defiantly regardless of any copyright of the title, his famous tooth-powder "Cherry Blossom," which was to "purify the breath, cleanse the teeth, harden the gums, renovate the teeth, stop decay, beautify the complexion," &c., and in general make life a paradise, all for the small sum of one penny a box. Occasionally a boy is had up from the crowd, and his teeth

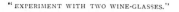

"EXPERIMENT WITH TWO WINE-GLASSES."

"THE GREATEST DOCTOR OF THE LONDON STREETS."

If he hadn't enough to last him a lifetime, he was apparently pretty well off, as his well-appointed pony and trap sufficiently testified.

But the open-air entertainments are, of course, if not more amusing, certainly more attractive to the crowd.

We have seen more than one very excellent conjuror at a street corner, and as it is necessarily more difficult to perform in the open with little or no apparatus, and the audience completely surrounding one, perhaps they may be entitled to some credit.

Guinea-pigs discovered under an old hat, which had the moment before been lifted to show its emptiness by a small wand held at tucked-up-sleeved arms' length, rapid manipulation with cups and marbles, card tricks neatly shown, and other feats of legerdemain are comprised in the street conjuror's programme.

Open-air recitations have become very prevalent of late years. Here is one who

cleaned for him with a small piece of wadding, though generally a fairly good specimen dentally is selected.

The writer once stopped to listen to another type of quack, more modestly served with the usual naphtha lamp and small box on stand. He was a man with a fierce eye and very sallow complexion, who rejoiced to find one of his audience at the time afflicted with face-ache or neuralgia. He had an instantaneous cure by inhalation, and, indeed, if unable to discover a face bound up with a handkerchief or some other apparent evidence of neuralgic pains, would boldly and thunderingly accuse any particular one of the listeners of sciatica, neuralgia, tic-douloureux, or some other complaint, to the blushing confusion and ineffable distress of the victim of his declaration.

Another gentleman, with every assurance, declared solemnly that he was not there for himself, he was working on behalf of a very dear friend laid on a bed of sickness. He (the quack) had made enough and plenty of money to last him all his lifetime, and, apparently forgetting what he had said before, was selling his herbal compound purely, solely, and simply for the benefit of the people.

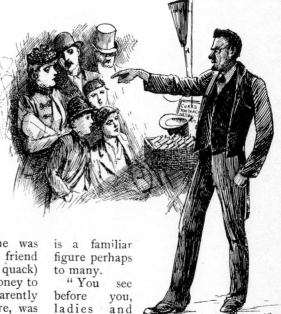

"AN INSTANTANEOUS CURE."

is a familiar figure perhaps to many.

"You see before you, ladies and gentlemen, a trained actorr

and accomplished el-o-cu-tionist, one who has travelled throughout the whole of the countries of Europe,

"A CONJUROR."

Asia, Africa, and America." It is no use, apparently, unless one is thorough in one's statements. "I have given recitations in the bleak frost-laden countries of Northern Russia and Siberiar, in the balmy climates of the South, the burning deserts of the East, and the wild backwoods of America, and for the small sum of 6d." (collected in advance) "will give you any recitation you chuse to harsk for, from Homah or Shakespeah down to George R. Sims. I require 6d. only, to get my night's lodging."

Nobody venturing to suggest a subject—or, if they do, it's about the same—our hero impressively gives out "Christmas Day in the Workhouse," by George R. Sims, fairly enough recited; at the conclusion of which another street-corner is sought for the same performance.

Another class of street-corner men are more of the "Cheap Jack" kind of individual. The wily lures of some of these gentlemen are not always discoverable by a cursory attention to their methods. Imagine coming upon a young fellow in a trap, with the usual flaming naphtha lamps, solemnly holding a boy whose head has a white kerchief over it, looking much like a small culprit prepared for the hangman,

and the said young fellow, with great volubility, explaining some extraordinary and curious phenomenon which would happen, if sufficient attention were paid, but of which it is impossible to make head or tail. This is the simple dodge to collect an audience. That once done, the handkerchief is whipped off, the boy nimbly jumps down, and a copy of *The Evening News and Post* is carefully scanned to point out the advertisement of the young fellow's master, who, purely for advertising purposes, has sent him to this street-corner to sell, or rather, give away, for the audience is emphatically assured that all money taken will be returned, the celebrated pure Abyssinian double electric gold rings to be had at his master's establishment only, at the advertised price of 1s. 4d. "I harsk only one penny from each person for one of these rings. I am not allowed to sell less than one dozen, the same as hadvertised at 1s. 4d." (here the advertisement in *The Evening News* is again referred to, this time the paper upside down ; but that is of no consequence) ; "and all those who purchase this ring, stay where you are ; don't go away."

The dozen disposed of, the purchasers are requested to hold up their hands, and the pennies are duly returned. So far, so good. The next article would be a magnificently chased, pure Abyssinian double electric keeper ring, looking sparklingly bright in the glare of the lamps, for which twopence is asked, though sold at the head establishment at 2s. 6d., and the purchasers are earnestly entreated not to go away. Obvious deduction, the twopence of course to be returned. Two dozen only allowed to be sold of these. When duly disposed of, and another dozen tried in defiance of the strict regulations, it is found with the very extreme of irrelevance that time does not permit of several gold and silver watches being given

"AN ACCOMPLISHED ELOCUTIONIST."

H. Tuck

away, so the "tuppences" are swept into the young fellow's pocket, to enable him, as he says, to give the audience another chance.

Diving quickly into a large box, paper packets are produced warranted to contain something, if only a bent wire button-hook, two of these being sold for 1d.

The sale slackening, one or two are opened, and out fall ivory-handled pocket knives, gold and silver alberts, brooches, &c. A fictitious rush thus created, divings into the box are rapid and frequent, with a large occurrence of bent wire button-hooks and waste-paper among the sold packets. Apparently the public rather enjoy the joke of this chance lottery.

We once came across a very good-

"A DODGE TO COLLECT AN AUDIENCE."

tempered-looking sort of Cheap-Jack who was selling for sixpence what he called the great Parisian novelty, a pocket knife that had a glazier's diamond in the head (with which he cut up quantities of glass), two blades, a file, scissors, corkscrew, gimlet, and goodness knows what besides; and he had in addition albums, scissors, plated spoons, and all kinds of domestic cutlery.

"What! Don't want no albums! Well, what shall I show yer? I've tried yer with everythink. But there, I hain't agoing to despair. I've got a little harticle here—I hain't a-going to tell yer no more lies to-night; if I do, may I be a teetotaler—I've got a little harticle here—and I've honly got a very few, so you'll have to be quick—a carver, carving fork, and steel, real Sheffield make, the maker's name stamped on the blade; none o' yer German-sausage manufacture, real English; a little harticle that, if yer wos to take 'em to Mappin's or Benetfink's, or any o' them there places, I tell yer, it would make them open their eyes. They'd tell yer they'd never seen such carvers before, and I dare say they never did. Now, who'll 'ave 'em? Eighteenpence, fifteen—'ere, a shillin'; who'll 'ave 'em? 'Ere, look 'ere, ninepence, eight-pence" (with a bang), "sixpence! Now who'll 'ave 'em? If I can't sell 'em to yer, I'll give 'em to yer. Fancy, 'ere's a present for the missus! Why, you'd be able to buy twice as much meat for yer Sunday's dinner; the carvers 'ud cut it up so quick; and, after dinner, you could sit at the winder and blow

"DOMESTIC CUTLERY."

yer bacca; and all for the small sum of sixpence! Now hain't that much better than sharpening hup the hold knife on the winder-sill in yer shirt sleeves, when the people's a-coming out o' church down below? Now, who'll 'ave 'em, honly sixpence, and I'll make yer a present of the sheet of paper they're wrapped in?"

And so he went on, when one article hung fire promptly introducing fresh ones.

Many other street-corner men there are; the sweetstuff man, for instance, who sells so rapidly that two boys are employed to open the bags for him—one penny a quarter of a pound—and occasionally mohair lace sellers, puzzle and toy retailers, shipwrecked mariners, street butchers, song sellers, negro entertainers, and others; but we have endeavoured, within the limits of this article, to indicate only some of the characters who make a speciality of a street-corner pitch, rather than the heterogeneous army of those who may be termed the kerbstone characters of the London streets.

"A SWEETSTUFF MAN."